THE MASQUERADES OF NIGERIA

AND

TOUCH

T0346611

Mask: A Release of Acting Resources

A series of books written and illustrated by David Griffiths

This book is part of a series. The publisher will accept continuation orders which may be cancelled at any time and which provide for automatic billing and shipping of each title in the series upon publication. Please write for details.

THE MASQUERADES OF NIGERIA

AND

TOUCH

Written and illustrated
by
David Griffiths

 Routledge
Taylor & Francis Group

LONDON AND NEW YORK

First published 1998
by Harwood Academic Publishers.
Reprinted 2004
by Routledge,
2 Park Square, Milton Park, Abingdon, Oxon, OX14 4RN

Transferred to Digital Printing 2004

Copyright © 1998 OPA (Overseas Publishers Association) Amsterdam B.V. Published under license under the Harwood Academic Publishers imprint, part of The Gordon and Breach Publishing Group.

All rights reserved.

No part of this book may be reproduced or utilized in any form or by any means, electronic or mechanical, including photocopying and recording, or by any information storage or retrieval system, without permission in writing from the publisher.

British Library Cataloguing in Publication Data

Griffiths, David
   The masquerades of Nigeria; and, Touch. – (Mask: a
     release of acting resources; v. 4)
   1. Masquerades – Nigeria
   I. Title   II. The masquerades of Nigeria
   792'.028' 09669

   ISBN 3-7186-5720-1

Applications for permission to perform *Touch* should be addressed to David Griffiths, Quaker Cottage, Quakers Lane, Rawdon, Leeds, LS19 6HU, England.

Cover illustrations by David Griffiths.

I dedicate this book to my late parents Jack and Doris,
who initiated and inspired the opportunity,
and to Vicky who supported me unselfishly throughout the period of
research and writing, and shared the joy of its completion.

CONTENTS

INTRODUCTION TO THE SERIES

Mask: A Release of Acting Resources is a fully illustrated four-volume series, which examines the effect of mask in performance.

This series reflects my practical work and draws upon my research into the secret world of the Noh of Japan and the Masquerade of Nigeria, the comic style of the Commedia Dell'Arte and the training of actors through mask in Britain.

The series also includes my three written masked plays called *The Dove, Please Be Gentle* and *Touch*, which transform and test the results of my experiments into theatrical practicality.

David Griffiths

ACKNOWLEDGEMENTS

I would like to thank the following: Dr David Richards for sowing the seed and making the original research enquiry on my behalf; the School of English, University of Leeds, for giving me the opportunity; the British Academy for setting the precedent of offering me an annual award and having faith that it would be used responsibly; Tom Needham for his friendship and his "investment" of £1000, without which I would not have been able to visit Japan; the Society of Friends for their grant of £500, which was given to me at a time great financial need; all those at the Tramshed in Glasgow who led me to *The Mahabharata* and Peter Brook; Chris and Vayu Banfield who have embraced me with a continuous stream of encouragement, practical help and invaluable advice; Alan Vaughan Williams, a wonderfully exciting theatre director, who gave me some of my early directing work and who continues to support and encourage without qualification; and Professor Martin Banham who supervised and guided me through my original enquiry with extreme care, the right amount of humour and encouraging portions of excitement.

In Japan, I am eternally grateful for the extraordinary hospitality and kindness given to me by my supervisor Professor Yasunari Takahashi, Jo Barnett CBE (Director of the British Council, Tokyo) and his staff at Kyoto, Chizuko and Naoichi Tsuyama my hosts and dear friends, Richard Emmert, and Fumiye Miho and Friends at the Friends' House in Tokyo.

LIST OF ILLUSTRATIONS

INTRODUCTION

In this final book in the series I shall describe the most important and significant practical experiment which I devised and conducted, to exemplify the theoretical description of the actor-training philosophy I described in Volume 1.

Had I not discovered the work of Wole Soyinka as a result of my attending the African Studies seminars at the University of Leeds, I would not have considered the Masquerade in this thesis. However, the more I read Soyinka's plays and marvelled at the quality of his dramaturgy, the more I delved into the influences which permeate the content and style of his work.

As I became familiar with the Masquerade, so I traced common links with the origins of the Commedia and especially the Noh. If I could reach such conclusions about the universality and influence of these masked dramas – then I felt confident that my philosophical argument was sound.

In order to finally test the validity of this theory I wrote a trilogy of short plays entitled *Touch* which were directly influenced by the masquerade elements explicity used in *A Dance of The Forests* by Wole Soyinka.

Like *Please Be Gentle*, the Touch trilogy was written to be performed within the particular framework of mask. The final play in the trilogy is played without mask although the acting style is explicitly influenced by the masked philosophy which has preceded it.

The Masquerade

As with the Noh and Commedia, the masqueraders are masked, and their appearance in the community is both expected and familiar. They and their dances and chants are known and are recognised to have a historical and ancestral lineage. Their sense of celebration is as much spiritual as it is theatrical and social.

Like the Noh, all those who are masked, and perform in the Masquerade represent ghosts; in this case, most specifically, of their dead ancestors.

They...

'leave their heavenly abode periodically to visit the human community. The belief in the periodical visitation of ancestors to the human communities is a common religious belief in most African societies.' [1]

Masqueraders are regarded as special people in their communities forming a crucial and fundamental link between past and present generations. Their methods of displaying and presenting their ancestry, is handed down with ritualistic care and thoroughness from generation to generation similar to the process described in the Noh.

Whereas the actors in the Noh devote their lives to the acquisition of skills which they will need if they are to survive the rigours and scrutiny of their profession, the masqueraders learn the theatrical skills as a means of taking on the correct and ritualistic form of their ancestral religion. They and their masquerades are fundamental to the spiritual well-being of their community.

They represent in fact the collective spirits of the ancestors who occupy a space in heaven. These ancestral spirits are believed to be in constant watch of their survivors on earth. They bless, protect, warn and punish their earthly relatives depending on how their relatives neglect or remember them. The ancestral spirits have collective functions that cut across lineage and family loyalty. They collectively protect the community against evil spirits, epidemics, famine, witchcraft and evil doers, ensuring the well-being, prosperity and productivity of the whole community generally. [2]

The presentation of the Masquerade as both a community religion and as a theatrical event has a familiar historical and social reference. It functions as an instructional instrument for a cultural philosophy, and is interpreted by artists both within and without the community as a means of preserving a strong belief in the philosophy for the benefit of that community.

Such a community is the Yoruba tribe of Nigeria, and such an artist is Wole Soyinka. Soyinka takes the Masquerade, its theatricality and its function in the Yoruba community, as one of the main thematic and theatrical resources for his play *A Dance of The Forests*. It is to this resource and the play that I shall address my enquiry.

Definition: The Masquerade

'Ancestral spirits may be invited to visit the earth physically in masques and such masquerades are also referred to as Egungun.' [3]

---

[1] Beir, U. A Year of Sacred Festivals in one Yoruba Town (*Nigeria Magazine,* 1959) pp. 26–29
[2] Babayemi, S. O. *Egungun Among the Yoruba* (Ibadan, 1980) p. 1
[3] Babayemi, S. O. p. 1

Like the Noh the 'performers' are entirely covered by their masks and costume.

1. Cloth mask   2. Carved headpiece

'As the corpse of the deceased is covered head and feet (from head to foot) so are the Egungun in heaven. That is why every Egungun is fully costumed, no part of the masquerader must be revealed to the public.' [4]

The head masks are made from a variety of materials, but are usually of fabric or wood. If it is carved, it may reveal instantly recognisable tribal markings, and hairstyles endemic to the lineage may be attached: it may represent a totemic animal or bird sacred to the family.

'For those lineages who do not use a wooden mask, the head of the masquerader is covered in layers of strips of material which move and spread accordingly as he dances. The costume of the lineage Egungun usually forms an extension of this type of headgear, having built into the design layer upon layer of heavily adorned strips of costly material; the quality and value of these strips indicating the financial status of the lineage.' [5]

---

[4] Babayemi, S. O. p. 6   [5] Babayemi, S. O. p. 35

Each lineage Egungun displays its own form of recognisable emblematic identification in terms of colour and design, and the place and status of each Egungun in their respective communities is measured by the response socially to this display.

> 'The identification of the various lineages that make up the corporate communities is very important for the individual in society as it is the passport for social and political recognition of a man. The more corporate and united a lineage is, the easier it is for the members to get suitors, as marriage in Yorubaland is more of a union of two lineages rather than the husband and wife.
>
> The outing of the lineage Egungun is one of the ways the Yoruba show the solidarity of their different lineages.'[6]

Each Egungun performer is bound by the detailed social conditions, rituals and historical traditions of his lineage. He is required and expected to place his special skills of lineage at the disposal of his community.

Many Egungun are part of a traditional lineage of masqueraders. They are prepared over a period of years by their ancestors. They learn songs and chants, dances and symbolic displays which recall the names and achievements of illustrious characters of the past, relaying to the living the historical example to which they should continually refer and emulate.

Each Masquerade follows its own ritualistic 'theatrical' format. However, the common factors of all masquerades usually includes an invocational drumming or horn playing in praise of the Egungun, which is then accompanied by the singing and chanting of the lineage women, and is designed to create an appropriately receptive state by those gathered in preparation for the arrival of the Egungun.

Once the Egungun appear they are expected to call at the homes of their immediate relatives to bless them and receive gifts, and also pause at specific places such as burial grounds, cross-roads, large compounds and ...

'display intricate and complex dancing steps.'[7]

Some Egungun only emerge at night and their presence is particularly identified by the sounds they make as they move, caused by the percussive metal pieces which are added to their costume and staff. Their faces must not be seen by ordinary men and women. Even the head of the compound, when offering gifts, greets the Egungun with his back facing him to avoid eye contact.

Finally, there are groups of Egungun who belong to no particular community but who perform their Masquerades as entertainments, and who sustain a livelihood by travelling from place to place using their particular

---

[6] Babayemi, S. O. p. 37   [7] Babayemi, S. O. p. 35

3. Masquerade and dancers

performing skills. They represent a form of professional Egungun, and are hired by heads and councils of communities to appear at specific festivals or celebrations, and are given a percentage of what is collected.

Their programme will usually include the familiar invocation of chants and drumming, and also poetry to which they set and display their special dancing skills. The following 'professional Egungun' quote could almost be associated with a Commedia performer.

> *'More than this, they compose songs on contemporary events... and on different lineages of the community.* [These will be commissioned and prepared in consultation with the council beforehand]. *They stage acrobatic displays and perform some tricks as if they are performing magic. They make people believe that they are communicating with the spirit world. They mimic different types of peoples and objects, hunters, imbeciles, prostitutes, white couples with their pointed noses embracing each other in public, monkeys, boas, the tortoise and the like. They usually expose the bane of the society in drama.'* [8]

So the arena of these celebrations follows a dramatic form which is not too dissimilar from those which have already been described in previous volumes.

---

[8] Babayemi, S. O. p. 39

4. Masquerade and dancers

The Masquerades of Nigeria display a highly animated ritualistic form of masked dancing, where the masks personify ghosts from the past, where evil is exorcised, where purification is invoked, where the spiritual, moral and cultural education of the existing community is redefined.

It is from this background that Wole Soyinka drew inspiration and created *A Dance of The Forests*, one of his most complex dramas. As a result of my reading this play, I became inquisitive about the form of the Masquerade, and in particular, the way in which its structure and purpose had influenced Soyinka.

A Dance of The Forests

A Dance of The Forests resonates with long lost, yet familiar chords of theatricality. I had discovered, quite by accident, a play and a form which recalled the epic spectrum of the Greeks, yet also embodied the more intimate detail found in the classical dramas of the European Renaissance. *A Dance of The Forests* is a play which evolves naturally from familiar celebratory rituals, inextricably linked with the very fabric of life in African communities.

Simple, worldly, and fundamental in concept, yet highly complex to those with little knowledge or experience of the richness of the language, history and texture of the Nigerian culture, *A Dance of The Forests* grips the imagination. In entertains the supernatural worlds of ghosts and gods, and yet is filled with the basic earthly reality of community living. Its themes and tone are perennial.

Set and performed for the first time in 1960, the year of Nigeria's Independence, it is written with this celebration very much in mind, and reveals Soyinka's appeal to his countrymen to take particular note of their new era of political and social responsibility.

His human accountancy makes very depressing reading; a catalogue of the wanton destruction of self and the environment. The only hope for the future of his country lies in man's truthful examination of the idyll of past eras, and of the desperate need to learn from them. By recreating his picture of the Yoruba cosmology he is recreating a microcosmic vision of humanity in general.

The power and poignancy of the opening to the play, displays a stunning command of visual theatre.

'An empty clearing in the forest. Suddenly the soil appears to be breaking and the head of the Dead Woman pushes its way up. Some distance from her another head begins to apppear, that of a man. They both come up slowly…. The man is fat and bloated, wears a dated warrior's outfit, now mouldy. The woman is pregnant. They come up, appear to listen. They do not seem to hear each other.' [9]

5. *A Dance of The Forests.* Dead Woman and Dead Man emerge from the soil

---

[9] Soyinka, W. *A Dance of The Forests* (Play text from *Collected Plays, I.* Oxford, 1973) p. 7

The play begins by introducing to us the first 'ghosts'. It contests the exchange between Man and the Gods and uses the traditional rituals of sacrifice and appeasement as a means of re-unification. Both Man and the Gods confront their own and each other, and are accountable for their actions.

By recreating his mythical and metaphysical past, and supplying his audience with a vision of the God's continuing presence and ensuing influence upon Man, Soyinka states the importance of the continuing availability of the historical, ancestral, spiritual, and celebratory reference for his discerning countrymen. Lessons must be learned from the past if Nigeria is to successfully effect this most vital period of transition, and must liaise with the old before a new state can be entered.

Even amidst his most pessimistic moments he positively indicates the way forward, making great play (perhaps egotistically!) upon the energy and integrity of the artist as being the most likely, influential visionary. As Gerald Moore said in his chapter on Soyinka in *Twelve African Writers*:

> 'In a world where most of mankind is blindly intent upon repeating the follies and crimes of the past, it is the hero/artist alone who hazards his own existence in one desperate effort to disturb the circle of fate, to alter in some way the repetitive pattern of events.' [10]

I don't wish to enter into a lengthy criticism of the play. I have described its general thematic content and made a brief contextual reference. But I would like to give a short synopsis of those aspects of the play which stimulated me and influenced directly my writing of the *Touch* trilogy.

Such is the density of the play in terms of characters and setting, of time and myth, as an example of social morality, that it was necessary for me to first of all break down its technical complexities into more accessible and simplified dramatic settings.

Because of Soyinka's strong narrative style I was able to conjure empty spaces of time and location in the imagination of the characters and thus the audience. I discovered many untold tales, and many possible lines of further exploration.

There were many characters and their relationships which seemed to speak directly to me and my culture; in particular the perennial question of human procreation, man's ever-changing attitudes to parenthood, and the way in which each generation is introduced and led into adulthood and society.

I was especially interested in the story of the Dead Man and the Woman, their unborn child carried across time, and its ultimate release

---

[10] Moore, G. *Twelve African Writers*: From Across the Primeval Gulf (Hutchinson, London, 1980) p. 218

from, and quick return to, the womb. The Half-Child and its brief glimpse and experience of humanity, fascinated me.

So did the stock representatives of Mankind, in the form of the artist, politician and prostitute, and their links with the Forest Dwellers the eternal spirits of time. Everything that happens in the forest is subject to the magical distortion of the unreal world, and yet within this mystery are revealed the clues for administering a stable and harmonious human landscape.

Whilst Soyinka introduces a Masquerade at the conclusion of the play, in order to point his political vision, there is a profound feeling in his description of characters and their enactment of events, that all the characters are masked, and are the recognisable re-incarnation of a previous ghostly and sometimes ghoulish life.

THE *TOUCH* TRILOGY

Losing Touch, the first play of the trilogy, is written for masked actors, and focuses upon the story of the Dead Man and Dead Woman, their unborn Half-Child and the fact that in their state of limbo – their single most psychologically damaging punishment – they can never touch each other.

I unashamedly echo the characters of Soyinka's play and his 'Soldier's Tale', and I used the Ashanti figure *(Shepherd)* as a kind of Prospero who functions as Chorus – in the classical sense – for most of the play, directing and commenting, shifting the story and emphasis as and when she sees fit; woman being displayed throughout the trilogy as storyteller, and therefore controller.

In the play, the wearying plight of the 'no touch' state of the *Him* and *Her* as they became animated, is quickly exemplified in anecdote and dance.

The trial scene was developed, and the 'touch' theme given a bitter re-enactment, as a device used for interrogation. The *Unborn* was released into the world and subjected to its influence, and returned to *Her* in its original state as a 'Half-Child' in limbo, being preferential to its temporary new-born condition.

The design of the acting space resembled that of a Noh theatre in scale and shape, though the square was turned through ninety degrees so that one of its corners pointed down stage and its opposite corner upstage. The traditional upstage 'bridge' entrance of Noh from upstage right, was replaced by a corridor of light stretching across the upstage corner of the square, from stage right to stage left. The floor space was covered like a boxing ring, with a calico cloth, and a 'sail' of similar material was hoisted during the uncovering of *Him* and *Her* remaining suspended above them for the duration of the play.

One or two portable cuboids were used to effect changes of location, and to provide different acting elevations. It has to be said that this design was conceived prior to my visit to Japan and my subsequent design for *The Dove* (see Volume 2).

The entire performance was accompanied by a complementary score of sounds and music, created on Sangbai drum and xylophone, played live by two African musicians. These sounds matched mood and movement of the protagonists, and contributed much to the authentic ethereal qualities of the spiritual environment surrounding the masks.

At its simplest, it recreated a basic narrative style of theatre where ...

SHEPHERD: *Here, in this space, anything, anything you like. There has to be a place like this for us to play, where anything can happen (CHUCKLES) take place. Because if there isn't, then we're finished; forget it! (QUIETER) But we're not – yet.**

Throughout the play the *Shepherd* continues to nudge and challenge the audience concerning the use of the acting square, and the manner in which she activates the 'magical' elements of character, action and location.

There is a strong influence of the Commedia technique which pervades the structure of many scenes.

Firstly, the stage is occupied mainly with duos and trios, and only rarely filled with the cast of eight. Throughout, all the seven speaking characters are positioned in the half-light, so that the audience is just aware of their presence in the acting square whilst they are not encountering each other. The three human characters are stock, and archetypal being a Prostitute, an Inquisitor and a Poet.

Secondly, all speaking characters wear half masks, influenced in their design by the textures, colours, and traditional shapes of a number of ceremonial masks made by Yoruba and Igbo mask-makers.

I have always been unhappy with the technical difficulties of articulation posed by the full mask based upon the mask designs of the Greeks and Romans. We don't know enough about the mouth shapes and the technical skills to present the characters vocally. Having seen the Noh, in rehearsal and performance I now have first hand knowledge of the technical skills required for full mask – and why I avoid it.

One mask, that of the Half-Child was a full mask. This is a non-speaking, mainly dance and mime part.

Thirdly there are many versions of lazzo, which help the protagonists especially, to key their physical rhythms and language to their mask and their dialogue. *Him* and *Her* for instance, spend the whole of the play, testing, being frustrated by, and reluctantly accepting their state of 'non-touching.' There are many 'set-pieces' of technical exchanges which establish their purgatory condition, and reveals their human frailty and forgetfulness, and the resulting pain.

The 'non-touching' unfulfilment of their suspended love state, is partly accommodated by their games of reminiscence. This provides for them and the audience another layer of animated story-telling. Their 'raven' dance is part of a perverse and cruel game and relates to a series of half-finished 'remembers'; all of this is watched and controlled by the *Shepherd*.

---

* See below, p. 24

Each 'lazzo' is technically structured in such a way that it offers the actors an unlimited range of rhythmical, physical action which will punctuate and complement the linguistic structure. Whilst it is 'structured' in the sense that the relative rhythms have to be adhered to very closely to find the keys to realise the complete clarity of the narratives and games, there is a wide spectrum of possibilities which enable different combinations of actors to recreate these 'lazzi' with a total conviction of freshness.

At the conclusion of the play, the Half-Child is released from the womb of the Dead Woman.

'Let this gourd, let this gourd
Break beyond my hearth...'[1]

For the first time we encounter the full mask of the Unborn. Its design is based upon the four to five-month face of an unborn foetus, although it inevitably contains identifiable features of the masks of Dead Man and Dead Woman. The actor's performance is almost totally choreographed as a masked dance, as there is no dialogue.

The scene changes are a crucial part of the choreography and the action. As with the Noh, time and location can change with a word; shifting forward and backward in time poses no problem for an audience cupped in the hands of a good storyteller.

SHEPHERD: So... We cannot alter history, only our perspective of it. Time past is time passed. But we can, in this gathering, allow our imaginations to imagine. What if, as my gift, their child – which is still clinging like a giant teardrop – were to break prematurely, in our imagination. What if this half-born child were to flourish? Would it reach its potential? Or will it, even in this half-born state, be like an already infected ear of corn amidst an aborted harvest?*

Out of Touch, the second play in the trilogy, includes a mask painted on the face of the actor playing the storyteller figure. Her role as Clown, in chorus, is somewhat different to the Shepherd character, in that she encourages the charges of her Institution to tell their story, to explore their backgrounds, to test their common factors as a process of discovery and therapy.

The themes of 'separateness' and 'no contact' are continued and adjusted, and the moral attitudes by western society towards motherhood, is challenged and developed.

The two mothers (the inmates) in the play are a Prostitute Joan and a Business Executive Beth. The rights of mothers concerning the care of their

---

[1] Soyinka, W. *A Dance of The Forests* p. 70
* See below, p. 42

children, and the haunting area of child-suffering and abuse is explored; whether or not in our present society, it is better for unborn children to remain where they are, they having no choice in the matter of conception and birth.

Technically, the play offers a half-way stage between the exaggerated animation of the mask, and the less animated but no less technically choreographed characterisation of an un-masked play.

Once again I employed commedia techniques. All three characters had to learn a three-ball juggle. A character could only speak in the light, when she was in possession of a ball. The whole lighting design was based upon this concept, so that the lights displayed an animated language of their own. Because of this, the physical rhythms of exchanges of dialogue had to be written in such a way that they made sense, but allowed for the technical display of juggling agility. The juggling became a kind of physical grammar and punctuation.

The opportunity for an animated narrative style in this play is divided equally between the two 'inmates' of the institution. Their babies have been removed from their care and the audience discovers why through a series of sharp exchanges, and monologues. All the time, with each exposition, the 'juggling factor' provides the visual, physical animation.

Another factor which I include in all plays is the vital importance of personal properties. In *Out of Touch* for instance, the Prostitute clings to a handbag which is crammed with the props and trinkets of her profession, whereas the Executive addresses her mind almost totally to her Filofax.

It is vital also that actors playing unmasked characters prepare and present their performance with the same attention to detailed physical characteristics, as if they were wearing a mask. This was the most difficult aspect of the experiment, and the consequence of this challenge for the actors is revealed in the final play of the trilogy, *In Touch*.

In Touch has a cast of three, two women and a man. They are unmasked. The play is opened simultaneously with the closing of the previous play. The Clown tosses the juggled balls one by one into an offstage space. As she moves away, a more dowdy clad version of the Clown enters juggling the same balls. She wears the mask of the Half-Child.

The Prostitute and the Executive meanwhile have been substituted by *Him* a dry-stone waller, and *Her* a teacher, parents of the *Sibling*. From the moment the Sibling removes the mask and her Clown costume, she takes on the mantle of storyteller, using her parents' story – from the first nervous contact to their almost deaths – to help her describe her own evolution, and how, throughout, she had no choice.

A whole 'score' of physical keys is provided for the actor to explore in this play; a physical choreography which is marked for consideration alongside the dialogue.

14

The overriding structural idea resembles the form and ritual of a boxing match. The corners offer a sanctuary, a base to return to. Whilst in the corners there is much preparation, much advice, much repair, much to reflect upon as each round unfolds and passes. The sibling acts as referee and second to each combatant.

Familiar patterns of movement that were initiated in preceding plays of the trilogy, reveal themselves. 'Ravens' and nervous games of introduction mirror the 'no touch' sequences of the mask in *Losing Touch*.

Beyond all of that, was the realisation that here is a trilogy which seemed to encapsulate in theatrical terms the whole philosophy of my original experiment. Once the mask has released the acting resources of the physical language of gesture to complement the grammatical and rhythmical structures of speech, then we can use these same resources and skills to support the performance of the unmasked actor.

TOUCH

INTRODUCTORY NOTES

Touch is a play in three parts about love and parenthood and of the limitless durability of the human spirit. For the convenience of identification I have given each part a title.

In the first part, *Losing Touch,* a dead man *Him* and his dead, pregnant wife, *Her,* are granted an opportunity to re-examine their lives on earth some seventy years after their death. They meet a *Poet,* a *Prostitute* and an *Inquisitor* in a special place (Their Imagination) and tell them their stories in the hope of being released from their burden.

In the second part, *Out of Touch,* a prostitute, *Joan,* and a business woman *Beth* are in an institution and are fighting to reclaim their children who have been removed from their custody. By meeting each other on the same territory with the same quest in mind, they discover some startling revelations about each other: all part of the therapy devised by the Clown.

In the final part, *In Touch,* we follow the story of two parents (*Him* and *Her*) – from pre-courtship to old age – as told by their daughter *(Sibling).* Here, the resolution to 'touch' is discovered.

Each part has its own director who oversees the space, the characters and the narrative. They temper the brutality, shuffle uneasily at the humour, and bring action impatiently into focus once the anecdotes begin to ramble.

Touch re-introduces the mystical theatre of mask, where anything can happen anywhere in the imagination, anything you like; where pictures are as important as words.

Characters

The *Shepherd, Clown* and *Sibling* are all storytellers. Their style of presentation changes with the plays and also according to their distinctive personalities. However, their common factor is the way in which they nudge and push the characters into action and effect changes in time and location. They ask some of the questions on behalf of the audience but don't demand answers to be delivered chapter and verse.

Him and *Her* dominate the action in the opening and concluding play. The full physical and emotional development of their love-match is challenged and explored across the two plays. The same actors should play these parts. In the same way, the human and public image of the *Prostitute* spans the first two plays.

I suggest that the actor playing the *Poet* in the first play becomes the *Clown* in the second, and similarly the actor playing the *Unborn/Inquisitor* plays the part of *Beth*.

The *Unborn* is ever-present, whether she is the physical duplication of her mother, controlling the final play as the part of the *Sibling*, or as a constant, unseen reference point in the second play. What she represents in terms of 'choice' pervades the trilogy.

The Masks

6. Him (Dead Man)   7. Her (Dead Woman)

20

8. Shepherd

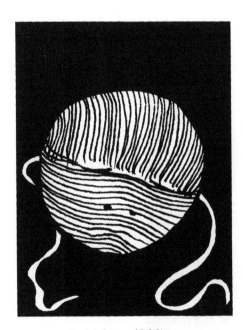

9. Unborn/Sibling

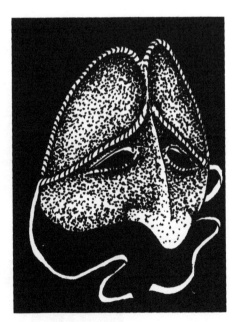

10. Poet

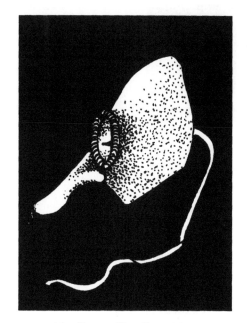

11. Counsellor/Inquisitor

12. Prostitute

13. Forest Demon

LOSING TOUCH

DEAD WOMAN: Better not to know the bearing
Better not to bear the weaning
I who grow the branded navel
Shudder at the visitation
Shall my breast again be severed
Again and yet again be severed
From its right and sanctity
Child, your hand is pure as sorrow
Free me of the endless burden
Let this gourd, let this gourd
Break beyond my hearth...
Wole Soyinka
(A Dance of The Forests)

CAST

SHEPHERD
HIM   The ghost of a soldier
HER   The ghost of his pregnant wife
SIBLING   Her *UNBORN* who becomes an *INQUISITOR*
PROSTITUTE
POET   Who becomes a *DOLL* who becomes a *CLOWN*.

Half masks are used in this first part. Their designs should be based upon the masks of the Yoruba of Nigeria, and should reflect the influence of the Masquerade.

THE SET

A twenty foot square acting area covered with unbleached calico, one corner running downstage into the audience. Upstage of the square, attached to the floor by one of its corners, is a similar square looking a bit like a huge dustsheet draped over three separate though closely related shapes – HIM, and UN-BORN seemingly stuck to HER in the same shape, sitting. They are not readily distinguishable as human forms though we suspect they are.

23

Between these two upper corners a two-body-width corridor of light runs from left to right and is the only route on and off the square.

Upstage of the cloths sit the musicians. Their music is used throughout to complement the action and in some instances provides motifs of identification to signal the entrance of a character.

The SHEPHERD enters slowly, carrying a thumbstick which she uses as she speaks to point her rhetoric. Her movements are rarely extravagant but always beautifully precise. She stops and looks at the audience carefully before speaking.

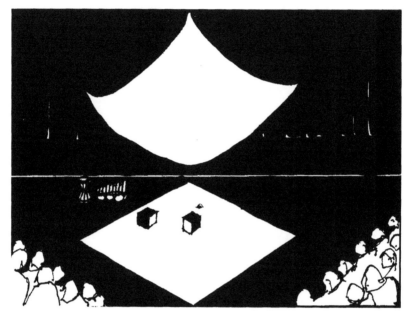

14. Set design for the *Touch* trilogy

SHEPHERD: Here, in this space, anything, anything you like. There has to be a place like this for us to play, where anything can happen, (*Chuckles*) take place. Because if there isn't then we're finished, forget it! (*Quieter*) But we're not – yet. There is an option. The snake can open its jaws and release its tail for a moment, and through the breach let out what is within (*Smiles*) or let in what is without. Like these. (*Indicates the three covered figures*) Been like this for over seventy years, thereabouts. Him, a soldier, captain. Her, his wife, like him, dead; unlike Him heavily pregnant. She, their unborn securely and resolutely attatched to her, goes with Her everywhere. No choice. Why are they here? Well now...

They are here because they are my guests, my ghosts. I have brought them back for you in my imagination so that we can (*Chuckles*) experience them, in this space. My choice not theirs. They have no choice. So... let's begin.

The SHEPHERD bangs her stick and a thin wire is lowered to which she attaches the downstage corner of the covering cloth, the sr and sl corners have been already set to similar wires. She bangs her stick again and the cloth is lifted by the wire until it opens and rests in the shape of a billowing sail. A rhomboid.

15. Opening sequence of *Losing Touch*

The Ghosts of HIM in tattered military uniform and a heavily pregnant HER are revealed sitting on small cuboids, and gradually lit... as Ghosts. Her pregnancy is not defined by a swollen stomach but by the ever presence of her UNBORN. Until there is an indication otherwise in the script, it is assumed that the UNBORN follows the movement of HER. This does not mean that the UNBORN's movement is exactly the same but mostly as though she is part of HER.

The SHEPHERD turns to the audience once again.

Let's see if, within this space, we can reach some measure of enlightenment (*Chuckles*) or not as the case may be. Got to be worth a try.

The SHEPHERD moves to the shadowy periphery beyond the square and stands, watching for a few seconds before banging her stick, activating HIM and HER.

HER: (*Struggling stiffly to sit upright muttering, very disgruntled*) What now? Always the same. As soon as I get comfortable you're wanting to shift me.
HIM: (*Stretching*) Didn't touch you.
HER: I know you didn't *touch* me
HIM: That's what you said.
HER: You know what I mean.
HIM: Never mind.
HER: Never mind?! I mind. Seventy Years I've been carrying this bloody thing, your thing. I mind allright. I want some peace.
HIM: (*Quietly*) So do I.

Enter the POET. He is closer to HER than HIM and she sees the poet first.

HER: (*Struggling to get to her feet*) Hello. 'Scuse me, er... you come to meet us? Thank God for that...
POET: (*Horrified at their appearance*) I'm sorry, I've not come to meet you. I'm a...
HER: But you must be here to meet us. There's no one else.
POET: I must go. Perhaps I'll meet you again when I've more time. (*Already moving away*) Goodbye...
HER: No! Please! we've only just arrived (*POET disappears*)! Please... (*SHE flops to a seating position again. The UNBORN clings heavily to her*)
HIM: (*Struggling to his feet*) That was clever. You frightened him to death. Poor sod took one look at you and ran.
HER: (*Outraged*) Me... ?
HIM: Well look at you.
HER: Me?
HIM: You you big mound.
HER: Have you any idea of what you look like?
HIM: Pretty impressive.
HER: Neither pretty nor impressive!
HIM: (*Feeling his face*) Well, maybe not but...
HER: Definitely not impressive! I can't help this... mound. (*Referring to her pregnant state*)
HIM: Your choice.
HER: Our choice.
HIM: Not again.
HER: Always again. You say the same thing every time. Whenever something rattles you I get the full blast of your rubbish.

HIM: And I'm rattled now?
HER: Yes.

(*Pause*)

HIM: (*Quietly*) Come on, get up.
HER: When I'm ready.
HIM: (*Moves closer to her*) Come on.
HER: When I'm ready! Don't you ever listen?
HIM: If we sit here doing nothing then we're wasting time. These are the only times that we can do something so... come on. (*Moves as though to assist her to her feet*)
HER: It's no good doing that. You can't touch me you oaf so don't try. For seventy years you've wasted your time trying. You're a bloody masochist as well as being an idiot!
HIM: (*Ignoring her jibes*) Try.
HER: (*Rolling onto her knees*) In my own time. I have to reconcile myself to my own time. (*Dips her head wearily*)
HIM: I know. But... I *feel* as though...
HER: Feel?!
HIM: Feel yes feel! I *feel* as though when I'm near you, like this, I can *will* you to do things, to *feel* things.
HER: Well you can't! It's up to me. It's no wonder I'm sick of you. You're perverse! (*HIM squats beside her*) And it's no good trying that. I can see what's in your mind before you've even thought it.
HIM: If we don't try then we've no chance. We stay as we are. Come on, make me laugh. If we can't laugh, we're dead.
HER: What are you saying ?
HIM: (*Smiling*) That you frighten me to death.
HER: And that's funny?
HIM: It's a start. (*Gently*) Come on you beautiful mound.

(*Pause*)

HER: My God you're ugly.
HIM: (*Grinning*) At last. Ready? (*Stretches out his arms as though to help her up*)
HER: No
HIM: Yes
HER: Not yet.
HIM: Yes
HER: In my own time. (*Preparing to stand*)
HIM: Yes
HER: Ugly sod!

HIM: How can you possibly say that?

HER: I have. (*She rises shakily to her feet*) You are. (*And stands rocking like a jelly until still. HIM tries to stabilise HER without touching*)

HIM: There.

HER: There.

Absolute stillness for say seven seconds

HIM: Ready?

HER: Not quite (*Shakes out her arms and flexes her shoulders*)

HIM: Ready?

HER: Nearly. (*More flexing. She is looser now*)

HIM: Now?

HER: (*Settles once again to a stillness. They are both preparing in fact for an embrace, one in which they will be locked together without touching*)
     Now. One.

HIM: One.

HER: Two.

HIM: Two.

HER: Three.

HIM: Three.

HER: (*Stopping. Coy. Wanting more coaxing*) Can't

HIM: Can.

HER: Not like this. (*Referring to unborn and her pregnant state*)

HIM: We've gone through all that. Try.

HER:: Can't. You know how it ends.

HIM: Doesn't matter.

HER: Can't

HIM: Doesn't matter. Do it.

HER: (*Swaying slightly*) Like this?

HIM: (*Instantly energised*) Like that. There. (*Begins to sway with her*)

HER: (*Settled*) There.

HIM: Ravens.

HER: Ravens.

THE RAVEN DANCE

SHE begins to wheel slowly in small circles, HE moves in a similar way about her. They take turns to 'Lead' the 'Touching' sequences whilst the other responds.

Gradually their clumsiness gives way to a grace and beauty as they spin a variety of 'Embraces' without actually touching.

As their dance develops, the early ecstacy of the ritual becomes more and more painful and frustrating as the reality of their lot once again dominates.

At its conclusion, emotionally exhausted, the response to each gentle touch looks like a response to the application of a high-voltage electrode. Their graceful beginnings become grotesque and slow and an air of resigned sadness prevails over their familiar frustration.

Their ultimate state of weariness is halted by the arrival of a prostitute who is totally absorbed in her self and the song she is singing.

PROSTITUTE: Oge, oge makam (*Time to myself*)
Ukwem ukwem (*My song my song*)
Kpochie isim na (*Blocking my head*)
Ukwem ukwem (*My song my song*)
Zapu inyi (*Clearing the filth*)
umu nwoke nine (*Of the last of the men*)
Kwado maka ozo (*Ready for more*)
Ukwem ukwem (*My song my song*)

Lua, lua tu onwem (*Work for myself*)
Ukwem ukwem (*My song my song*)
Welu isim na (*Using my head*)
Ukwem ukwem (*My song my song*)
Nye nkem chola (*Giving what I want*)
Nye ya ofuma (*And doing it well*)
Ka obalum (*Coining it in*)
Ukwem ukwem (*My song my song*)

Debe, debe lu onwem (*Keep for myself*)
Ukwem ukwem (*My song my song*)
Welu onwem na (*Using myself*)
Ukwem ukwem (*My song my song*)
Tupu nkaa (*Before I grow old*)
Uka arum yosia (*And the folds of my life hang from my skin*)
Ukwem ukwem (*My song my song*)

HIM and HER have moved apart HIM being closer to the prostitute than her. They are however caught in backlight and appear at first in silhouette to the PROSTITUTE.

HIM: Are you the one?

The SHEPHERD bangs her stick to freeze the action and moves quickly between the couple and the PROSTITUTE.

SHEPHERD: Now there's a question. (*Bangs her stick to activate the action*)

PROSTITUTE: (*Provocatively*) Depends. (*Bangs her stick to freeze the action*)

SHEPHERD: There's an answer. (*Chuckles*) And I still haven't told you why they are here, these ghosts. Well, each year, since their death seventy four seventy five years ago, I've invited them back, in my imagination, so that they can look at what they left and... comment on what they find. Learn something. Simple really. Unfortunately they're still preoccupied with self. Which is why I continue to punish them for their own good – gently of course. At this moment they have another chance to change their state. She (*Indicates the PROSTITUTE*) is a Prostitute. Like them outcast, outside. Little test. (*Moves away from the others, turns to face them and activates them by banging her stick*)

PROSTITUTE: Depends.

HIM: On what?

PROSTITUTE: On what you want. More important what you're prepared to pay. I can do anything.

HER: Anything?

PROSTITUTE: Who's she?

HER: Never mind who I am. You said you could do anything.

PROSTITUTE: Not for you. Him.

HER: Then you're no good to us. (*Turns to HIM*) waste of time.

SHEPHERD: (*Banging stick. Freeze*) Come on you can do better than that. That's too easy! (*Banging stick. Activate*)

PROSTITUTE: Who's she?

HIM: My wife.

PROSTITUTE: Then you definitely don't need me.

HIM: We both need you.

HER: Just a minute. (*Moves into light revealing her condition*) I know you.

PROSTITUTE: Not me. (*Repulsed*) Oh my God. No I definitely don't know you. Never seen you before in my life.

HER: (*Staggers threateningly forward*) I know you.

PROSTITUTE: You're disgusting. I mean just look at you!

HER: (*To him*) Look.

HIM: (*Moving into the light*) What?

HER: (*Quietly*) Look. (*Starts weeping*) After all that time. After all these tears. Her.

HIM: It's not.

HER: It is. Look at her.

HIM: It *can't* be.

PROSTITUTE: Hilarious. I don't believe it. (*Touching her head mocking*) You're stupid. (*Starts laughing*) Look you berk. You, are, re-vol-ting. Him, the most re-vol-ting looking man I've ever seen. Eeyuck! You're quite safe with him. In fact I think you're quite safe with each other. No one's going to touch either of you.

HER: But you did.

PROSTITUTE: You what? I'm off. (*Starts moving away*)

SHEPHERD: (*Bangs stick. Freeze. Angry*) Not yet !
(*Bangs stick. Activate. Quieter*) Not yet.
PROSTITUTE settles and turns to face HIM and HER

PROSTITUTE: Look. It's quite simple. I've never seen either of you in my life.

HER: But in *our* life (*Touches her head*) in here, you are locked like a maggot. And the further we drift in time the more you grow.

PROSTITUTE: You poor sod.

HER: Don't you remember the trial?

PROSTITUTE: Not with you two I don't. And believe me I don't forget many faces. You've got it wrong.

HER: Putting your hands all over him. In front of me?

HIM: She's right. You've got it wrong love.

PROSTITUTE: Definitely not me. I wouldn't even touch him with gloves on. I play around sometimes, course I do, part of the job but... eeyuck!

HIM: (*Comforting*) It wasn't her. It can't be her. She's here, now. (*To the PROSTITUTE*) I'm sorry.

HER: (*Disappointed*) But if it wasn't her it was someone just like her. I've had enough.

HIM: No.

HER: (*Starts walking away*) Enough.

PROSTITUTE: (*Moving in the opposite direction*) I know what you mean.

SHEPHERD: (*Spitting anger. Banging her stick. Freezing the action*) No! *Use* her, Persuade her to stay. She's all you have at this moment. Tell her the story. Try and *engage* her so that she understands something. When you've told her your story then she may shed a new light, she may. Don't forget, here... anything. Right? (*HIM and HER nod wearily*). Right. Persuade her to listen to your story. You begin.

HIM: How?

SHEPHERD: Simple.

HIM: But how?

SHEPHERD: Straight to the point. (*Bangs stick releasing the action*)

HIM: (*To the Prostitute*) Would you stay a minute and listen to our story?

SHEPHERD: That's straight enough.

PROSTITUTE: I came out here for a bit of peace and I have to meet up with a couple of dossers like you two. I got to go. (*Makes as if to move off. SHEPHERD bangs stick freezing the action*)

HER: Told you.

SHEPHERD: Last chance.

HER: What's the point?

SHEPHERD: Last chance.

HIM: Please.

SHEPHERD: (*Banging stick releasing the action*) Last chance.

HIM: Please.

PROSTITUTE: (*Takes another step and stops, turning slowly*) Five minutes. Five minutes that's all.

HIM: That's all we need.

PROSTITUTE: Five minutes and not a second more then I'm gone. End of it. Right?

HIM: Right.

PROSTITUTE: Right.

HIM: Right.

PROSTITUTE: Well get on with it.

HIM: Right. (*Suddenly brighter*) Right ! (*Turns to her*)

HER: Can't

HIM: You can. You always do.

HER: Too upset.

HIM: We're wasting time.

HER: I know how to do that.

HIM: I'll do it.

HER: You can't.

HIM: I'm going to.

HER: You take too long. You exaggerate. Take her round the Mulberry Bush.

PROSTITUTE: No chance. A minute gone already.

HER: Alright! Imagine. Imagine Him standing there. Naked.

HIM: Where?

HER: There. (*Nods to the centre of the square*)

HIM: (*Moving to the centre*) Right. (*Suddenly energised standing younger*) I'm here. Naked. Imagine that.

PROSTITUTE: I daren't. I'd be sick!

HER: Seventy years ago. Here then, here now. A beautiful man. Beaten and bent with weeks of manhandling. Not a bit of his body left untouched by the boot or baton of terrified guards apologising while they were doing it. So there he is, miraculously still standing. Hands tied. They still tied his hands. And the questions come at him slowly at first.

She gently releases her UNBORN who takes on the role of INQUISITOR and pushes her away from her.

Relax. Let's try again. You are very successful. Your losses are minimal and your victories many.

HIM: (*Closing his eyes, inclining his head as though covered with an opaque bag*) I am a professional soldier. I do my job.

HER AND UNBORN: Well let's say that you conduct yourself *professionally* with greater skill than most if not all of your fellow officers.

HIM: I wouldn't say that.

UNBORN: I would. We all would. You are – what is the word? – *invaluable* to us, to the whole nation. We really want you to change your mind.
HIM: No.
UNBORN: Well let's examine the logic of your argument.

Satisfied that her UNBORN is taking over her persona as inquisitor, HER moves back a couple of paces, and lowers her head standing silently and very still

You've killed many times. Correct?
HIM: Yes.
UNBORN: Without question?
HIM: Yes.
UNBORN: As a professional you are conditioned to obey. You were under orders?
HIM: Yes.
UNBORN: All of your victims were a sad but necessary sacrifice for the greater freedoms which you were striving to preserve – apart from the more immediate problems of self-preservation?
HIM: No. Wrong...
UNBORN: In all these situations as a highly trained... *man*, you have personally been responsible for thousands of deaths.
HIM: Yes...
UNBORN: Then why do you stop now, at this particular moment? Why do you suddenly decide to stop what you were trained to do. What you've cost us a lot of money to train you to do.
HIM: A human accountancy?
UNBORN: If you like, yes.
HIM: Simple. I withdraw my account. No more.

HE breaks from the inquisition attitude and looks for the SHEPHERD. As he does so the UNBORN rushes to HER and adopts her attitude of extreme concern. This all happens in a flash. The SHEPHERD bangs his stick quieter this time, freezing the action

HER: (*Desperate*) I've run out of time. I know I have.
SHEPHERD: Carry on. See, she's hooked. Time in suspense.
HER: You sure?
SHEPHERD: Sure. (*Bangs stick*)
HER: It's not as simple as that. I wish it were. (*Unfolds her UNBORN as before and pushes her forward as before to continue the inquisition, hesitant at first*)
UNBORN: Look, let's suppose you were injured and... unable to function as Captain. Even if you suffered from 'fatigue' – and God only knows that you must have – I mean if you couldn't ligitimately function... properly. No problem. Easy. Home for as long as you needed. No problem (*Pause*)

But there is nothing, nothing remotely like that to cling to. You're as mentally and physically sound as the first moment you joined us. Your file says you are in excellent shape, (*Chuckles*) so it must be true.

HIM: And my spirit?

UNBORN: (*Incredulous*) Your what?

HIM: My spirit. What reference is there in my file to my spirit. Does it say that I am in good heart, does it? Is it naive to hope that there is something in my file which measures not only my performance but how I feel about my performance?

UNBORN: (*Long pause*) Right. These are the words of others. These are not my words.

HIM: Then why use them.

UNBORN: I pass them on.

HIM: A real soldier.

UNBORN: (*Ignoring. Head inclined as though reading*) It is well acknowledged that you are the only man for this particular task.

HIM: (*Bored*) Not true. There are others. There are always others.

UNBORN: You have the respect of your men. (*Scornful*) Like disciples. Almost blind faith I would say.

HIM: Faith is faith. No definition needed.

UNBORN: Your leadership in this campaign would guarantee success and would ensure our overall supremacy. It would be sweet victory.

HIM: Sweet death. I am stuffed with death, sick with it. To kill more generations of other men, and women and... children... Not one more death will I be responsible for.

UNBORN: And you have no reason?

HIM: (*Shaking his head incredulous*) Reason enough I think.

UNBORN: Ah. Then it has nothing to do with reasons more domestic?

HIM: What sort of a meaningless comment is that?

UNBORN: No, seriously. Those at home. Your wife and child.

HIM: We have no children.

UNBORN: Not yet. But you will, soon. Hasn't your wife told you, yet. Four months gone. Half way. Solid as a rock. She's as fit as you and very committed. No, it's more a case of leaving her like she is. Let's look at it another way. (*She stops for a moment and drops her shoulders*)

HIM: (*Suddenly weary*) Go on love. Finish it.

HER: (*Wearily*) Can't.

HIM: You can. She'll disappear and we've lost another opportunity to finish it. Try.

HER: (*Falteringly at first but growing in power as she remembers talking now directly to the PROSTITUTE*) He said... he said to him.

UNBORN: (*Straightening, inquisitor again*) Let's look at it another way.

HER: And they turned him to face the door which led into the room where I'd been sitting through all of this with a bag over my head and said...

UNBORN: Let's look at your wife (*She moves slowly to HER and joins once again in her original role as attached UNBORN*)

HIM: You bastard !

HER: He said.

HIM: She has nothing to do with this! You dare bring her into this gutter. You bastard!

HER: He said all of that. And they led me into the room... (*She moves just beyond touching distance facing HIM*)... and stopped me here. Just here. And held us both very tightly, and removed the bags. (*They lift their heads facing each other*) And there we were looking at each other. Just out of reach. The last time we'd touched each other had been four months before that, just before he'd gone away.

If he'd not come back, if he'd been killed I could have coped. But this was beyond my imagination, out of my mind. And the next bit, your bit...

PROSTITUTE: My bit?

HER: Your bit. You swayed in and swished around...

PROSTITUTE: (*Surprised*) Me?

HER: You. They used you even though they knew they'd lost him. They couldn't face that kind of humiliation so they shat on him, by using you... and me. Come here.

PROSTITUTE: You what?

HER: If you want to know, stand there, behind him. Nearly the end of the story, of us. Won't take long.

PROSTITUTE: (*With a 'why not' shrug she moves into position behind him*) Here?

HER: Bit closer.

PROSTITUTE: (*She moves closer*) This do?

HER: That will do. Now... (*turns to him*) Sit down

HIM: Go away.

HER indicates that the PROSTITUTE takes over the inquisition. Amused she does with relish. She's used to games.

SHEPHERD: (*Bangs stick freezing the action*) Seventy years ago. No choice. (*Bangs stick releasing the action*)

PROSTITUTE: Oh dear. You have got a problem haven't you. (*He sits as if he's been forced to do so and his arms and legs are spread out as though tied back*) That's better. But I'm still very worried. This... (*Chuckles*) pacifism worries me very much. So... what can we do? How can I succeed where others have found you (*Smiles*) very difficult. (*She reaches out to touch him*)

HER: (*Turning away*) Enough.

PROSTITUTE: Don't do that lady you'll miss out. I've got some work to do on your husband. He's very unusual, your husband. Although he's very brave he is also very stupid. And it is very very important that his stupidity doesn't run around willy nilly amongst the underlings, unchallenged. Somehow or other I've got to convince him of this and restore our admiration of his worth. So, what I'm going to do is to reach out and take his hand and 'touch' him.

She takes his fingers and begins to touch the tips. Because the wrist is anchored the fingers open and snap in vain at the teasing hand of the amused PROSTITUTE like the snarling jaw of a desperate snared animal.

(*To Her*) You're not watching. Well that's up to you. How you watch is in your head. (*To Him*) All I can say to you is, that if you don't like me touching you, all you have to do is say so otherwise I'll assume that you like it very much. No? Then I'm going to touch you there (*Strokes one cheek, the head rigid as though clamped*) and there (*Strokes the other cheek*) and there (*Begins to move down to his chest*) doesn't matter where, where is never important... I'm going to touch you a lot, gently, softly, touching...
HIM: (*Quietly yet with total finality*) No.

The SHEPHERD bangs her stick and arrests the action

SHEPHERD: Enough. We don't want to watch them do we? Not when we have our imagination. (*Chuckling slightly*) Remember he's naked. To watch them really would be perverse wouldn't it? Time to finish the story, as it was, and see if anything has shifted. They can all help with this, including the Poet. Can't have him passing by as though he hasn't been touched can we? Poets shouldn't do that. So...

Bangs her stick and activates the group drawing our attention to the entrance of the POET who walks slowly to a prominant position as the SHEPHERD retreats to the shadows

SHEPHERD: Listen. Listen to the poet...

During the poem the four characters in the drama move slowly and rhythmically addressing their words carefully and directly to all the audience when they have the lines. They act as chorus to the others when they are silent. Everything gentle and hypnotic yet as clearly and sharply articulated as a wire cutting through cheese.

POET: When she knew, as she did,
    As she passed her hands
    Over the hollow, shuddering skin

Of his stretched, military frame,
And when she saw the knowing eyes
Of the hunched, mother – blown wife – love,
And knew there was no less resolve there
Than battles passed by both of them,
She turned her back
With her legs and her arms fixed
In the ridiculed crucifix
Of a dead-bellied, tortoise-shelled whore
And decreed that...

PROSTITUTE:

(*Quietly*) This man be cut
Where the pig is cut
And after, locked
In the dank sewers beneath our land,
To play with
Matchstick graffiti
Marking time
Until his cause is bloated enough
For future generations to gorge

POET: At this, the military man
Levelled unblinking at his wife – love
And searched in silence, in vain
For the simple understanding
Which he knew could never be there.
And when the whore
Had retracted her limbs
And turned her scorn
To petrify her next victim
The wife – love
Gathered her wretched body
And in a voice
So low, yet so clear
That even the bats
In their shrieking
heeling and dealing
Could not fail to hear,
Said...

HER: When we meet,
And spin around
The curling foam
Of drifting tides
Together, unable
To fold about each other

Soothing our emptiness,
May we reflect
That this conception
Was our choice,
And this life – form inside me
Was our choice,
And that my death inside me
Will deny also
This child, its life, its choice;
Then,
May we reflect upon that.
POET: And she turned
And left her military man
Untouched
Unkissed
And killed herself.

(Pause – say five seconds. The PROSTITUTE and POET move to the shadows and turn into the action)

SHEPHERD: (*Bangs her stick freezing the movement*) Now that we all know a little more of who they are and why they are here, it remains for me to decide whether they are ready to be released temporarily from their state, in our imagination. But before we do that, a little moment of lightness.

Sometimes – if sometimes can still be measured in time after so much time has passed – these two look over their bent shoulders and reminisce, as a means of coping: little touching stories. One of them begins, and the other catches it, in the air, and after a little cajolling while, joins in. This time it's her. (*Retires to the shadows and then bangs her stick to release the action*)
HER: Come on.
HIM: Come on what?
HER: Come on.
HIM: What?!
HER: Don't shout.
HIM: (*Quieter*) I'm not shouting.
HER: (*Quietly*) But you were. You did

Pause

HIM: (*Quietly*) But I'm not.
HER: So come on.

Pause

HIM: Now?

HER: Here. (*Looks around, checking*) No one to see.

HIM: What if they do?

HER: What?

HIM: Unexpectedly.

HER: What?

HIM: (*Smilingly*) Peek.

HER: Ignore them.

HIM: What?

HER: (*Glum*) Doesn't matter. (*Pause. Quiet. Sad*) I need to. I can't remember. I can't remember when we last did it, and if I can't remember then I'm done for, finished. (*Begins weeping quietly*)

SHEPHERD: (*Bangs stick freezing the action, irritated*) Wrong mood altogether. Enough of that. Brighter. (*Bangs stick animating the action*) Brighter!

HIM: (*Brightly*) Allright. Me first.

HER: (*Brightly*) Allright.

(*Long pause while he thinks*)

HIM: Er... nothing at the moment, I'm still (*Exaggerated thinking gestures*) thinking. So erm... (*Hands over the thinking gestures to her*) you.

HER: (*Enthusiastically receiving them*) Er... (*Nothing also. Pause while she thinks. Begins brightly, inspired*) It was long ago, long long ago, and it was a long long time ago when... (*Drops her shoulders enthusiasm eroded. Angry*) Forget it. All been done before.

SHEPHERD: (*Bangs stick*) Get on. Shift it. Now!

HIM: (*Suddenly lifting his head, brightly*) Remember, when we were walking, on the road, before we were married. Bread and Breakfast. (*Laughs*) Mr and Mrs Gale.

HER: (*Lifting her head. Brightly*) My name.

HIM: What?

HER: I invented it. First thing which came into my head.

HIM: What?

HER: We were soaked to the skin. Like a tempest it was. Wind, rain beating our ears. We stood on the doorstep and the landlady asked us our name and I said Gale...

HIM: The first thing that came into your head.

HER: Right.

HIM: Wrong. That was after.

HER: (*Relaxed*) I know. I remember.

39

HIM: Good.

SHEPHERD: (*Banging stick*) Good (*Banging stick*)

HIM: (*Warming to his task*) Right. Beautiful day. Sun shining, birds at it, Worker bees humming from Bramble to Sweet Briar. Paradise.

HER: I know. I remember.

SHEPHERD: (*Banging stick*) Good! (*Banging stick*)

HIM: We were walking down a steep lane, Hazel hedges laid on either side, Tarmac bubbling. (*Chuckles*) Brer Fox and the Tar Baby...

HER: (*Excitement gone*) No. We can't do that.

HIM: What?

HER: Stick to each other.

SHEPHERD: (*Bangs stick impatiently*) No! Get on with it, go forward. (*Bangs stick*)

HIM: (*Very excited*) Walking. On the left – the other side – two churns on sleepers wedged into the high bank, at the end of a long track leading to a farmhouse.

HER: Stop.

HIM: What?

HER: We stopped.

SHEPHERD bangs his stick more gently this time freezing the action – as though dramatising the 'stop' created naturally in the narrative. Waits for say four seconds before banging it in the same way to animate the action.

HIM: We did.

HER: Stopped and (*Pauses for a few seconds thinking very hard. Then brightly, remembering...*) crossed over.

HIM: Yes.

HER: Climbed up the bank.

HIM: No.

HER: (*Insistent*) Climbed up the bank beside the...

HIM: No! (*She is about to repeat the same detail of the story but she stops, very agitated. Thinks. Clams down her spirits visibly uplifted again. Gently*) No.

HER: No. I went to the gate.

HIM: (*Relieved*) Yes.

HER: Lookout.

HIM: Yes.

HER: (*Confident again*) Detail. Important. Lest we forget.

HIM: (*Chuckling*) Lest.

SHEPHERD: (*Banging the stick sharply*) On! (*Banging the stick sharply*)

Next exchange of animated dialogue almost pure commedia. Real beautiful little double-act lazzo

HER: No one coming (*They look*) no one about.

HIM: Check again.

HER: No one... in the yard (*They check*) on the track (*They check*) up the road (*They check*) skulking behind the hedge (*He has left her and meets her head on frightening her to death*) Aaah! You bloody idiot! Frightened me to death. (*They pause for a couple of seconds before exploding into laughter*)

Instant crack of the stick by the SHEPHERD stops the laughter. Another crack re-animates the action and the story rushes on. HIM and HER are nose to nose.

HIM: No one.

HER: Right. Ready?

HIM: Yes.

HER: Lift up the lid.

HIM: (*Whispering*) Knock on the can first.

HER: (*Laughing whisper*)What you whispering for?

HIM: So I can listen.

HER: (*Understanding*) Ah... Knock on the can, listen to the dong.

HIM: (*Knocking. Listening*) No echo.

HER: No echo (*Chuckling*) no dong.

BOTH: Full!

HIM: Now... You do it.

HER: No. You first. If they catch you, you've done it not me.

HIM: Doesn't make any difference. You've watched me. Just as guilty. Only difference is...

HER: You'll have guzzled a handful of cream and I won't.

HIM: Yes.

HER: (*Pause*) Me first.

HIM: OK.

HER: Lift the lid, hand inside, *finger* inside... (*Miming her index finger gently stirring the cream*)

HIM: (*Excited*) Yes?

HER: Feel it. Warm, soft mmm...

HIM: (*Very excited*) Yes?

HER: Cream.

HIM: Yes!

HER: mmm...

HIM: Go on. All of them. Dip all of them. Handful.

Unfolds her other fingers and spreads them gently stirring the cream. She pulls her hand dripping with cream out of the churn and offers it to HIM

HER: Here.

HIM: (*Moving towards HER focussed on the outstretched hand. Unthinking.*) Yes!

HER: Love it.

HIM: (*Almost touching it with his tongue. Stops. Rigid*) You...

HER: (*Still offering fingers*) Lovely.

HIM: (*Head and shoulders drop*) You...

HER: What's the matter? (*Sucks her fingers one by one*) Mmm, Lovely. Remember?

HIM: Yes.

HER: (*Stops suddenly dropping her hand*) Oh love. I didn't mean that I wanted you to...

HIM: But it felt like it.

HER: I was just happy...

HIM: I know.

HER: To be able to remember.

HIM: I know.

HER: What it felt like. It felt as though it were happening even though we were unable to...

Pause

HER: And that's good.

HIM: Good?

HER: Yes.

HIM: (*Stronger*) Good?

HER: Yes. Because we haven't lost the need to touch.

A long wail of frustration from HIM broken only by HER conciliatory attempt to calm and console. All arms and legs similar to the Raven Sequence earlier, unable to embrace. The reality of limbo. It is stopped by the SHEPHERD banging his stick.

SHEPHERD: Should have stopped it long before. However, we have shifted a little. At least she has. I'm going to remove him for the moment, put him back where he was. There's nothing more we do with him or his impotence, for the moment.

HIM walks, shoulders hunched, back to his place beneath the sail and settles into his original state. HER settles abjectly into the shadows turning away from the centre of light. The SHEPHERD watches him and turns slowly addressing the audience more directly, with a greater urgency.

So... we cannot alter history, only our perspective of it. Time past is time passed. But we can, in this gathering allow our imaginations to imagine.

What if, as my gift, their child – which is still clinging like a giant teardrop – were to break prematurely, in our imagination. What if this half-born child were to flourish? Would it reach its potential?

Or would it, even in this half-born state, already be like an infected ear of corn amidst an aborted harvest?

Let the dance begin and play out, here, in this space, its part, in this first part of this. Just... here.

The SHEPHERD moves slowly away from the centre of the square and stands at its upper corner.

HER moves towards and stands facing the SHEPHERD.

The SHEPHERD then lifts her arms. As she does so a LIVING DOLL FACSIMILE of the unborn seems to appear from within the folds of the shepherd's cloak – like magic.

The living doll holds hands with the UNBORN who is in turn eased gently into the square by HER. UNBORN tries to cling to her, but is released. She clings to her doll and is reluctant to go, puzzled, bewildered and terrified by her enforced separation.

Once the final rejection takes place UNBORN wanders alone.

In doing so she experiences the world and becomes influenced by its familiar characteristics of greed and bullying isolation, of self-preservation and deceit as she searches for love.

She discovers this during her meeting with the PROSTITUTE and IN-QUISITOR. She feels that love is there somewhere but she can't find it because they are not able to offer it.

She sets her doll temporarily aside and with tired resignation, she learns and adopts the survival characteristics offered by the PROSTITUTE and IN-QUISITOR dancing until she is exhausted. Once they have gone, she joins her doll and clutches it for comfort.

Eventually she begins to play with her doll. We watch her shape the doll's movements reproducing those she has just learned.

While she is in the middle of this process the SHEPHERD removes the doll, takes the UNBORN by the hand and leads her back to HER who wearily accepts her burden and slowly exits along the corridor of light followed by HIM.

The SHEPHERD releases the DOLL who quickly shifts the cuboids into position for the next play. DOLL seems to disappear into his cloak as he exits slowly following in the same direction as HIM and HER.

As SHEPHERD is about to leave the set, from the opposite side, along the corridor of light, the CLOWN appears, juggling.

Music Note

In the original workshop the African musicians used a variety of sangbai drums, and a xylophone with wooden keys and gourds. They devised simple motifs to introduce characters and to complement changes in mood. They remained unobtrusive in the sense that you were aware of their presence only when they stopped playing: these motifs became part of the music for the dance.

In the second and third play of the trilogy the motifs appear only occasionally to underpin the action and remind the audience of links in theme from this play.

OUT OF TOUCH

CAST

BETH: Business executive and mother
JOAN: Prostitute and mother
CLOWN

THE SET

Two cuboids which have been set at the conclusion of Losing Touch. They are separate but central to the empty square, one slightly downstage of the other.

CLOWN enters juggling three balls with consummate ease, along the corridor of light. The light highlights the balls more than her body. She is 'smiling' at the audience. After say ten seconds, she begins to speak slowly, quietly, using the rhythm and the soft 'touching' sound of the juggling to point the rhythm of the dialogue.

16. Clown

CLOWN: Once you know how, once you've been... taught... it's easy. Switch off. Passing through the air... hardly... touching. No... contact. If you start to feel... what you're... touching *(Starts moving backwards into the corridor of light)*... then it's all... fall... *(Lets two balls drop. Keeps looking at the audience for say three seconds, and then suddenly turns her head to signal the entrance of BETH along the same corridor of light. She tosses a ball into the wings. BETH emerges having caught the ball)* Beth.

(BETH is wearing the plain smock of an institution. She carries a bulging filofax diary, her only obvious possession. The CLOWN moves away from her out of light,

45

and adopts a standing posture which is both comfortable and yet professionally inquisitive.)

17. Beth

(Quietly re-introducing) Beth

BETH: *(Opening her filofax. Settles on a page and reads)* 'The 10th. Meeting with designers at 9:30. Sign letters John typed last night. Ring... National Parks, Young Farmers Appletreewick, Foster Quarries and... InterFlora, see notes "J". *(Flips to the back of her book)* O. P. J... Janet/James. James. Crysanthemums... Diary: The tenth. 'I will not have it!'

(Pause. Quietly) 'Desperate' *(Pause)* 'Hospital' *(Notices balls. Picks one up.*

As she does so the lights change focussing upon BETH but not quite isolating her from the CLOWN who is now also clearly visible. She shows no surprise.

CLOWN: *(Quietly)* Thank you *(Indicates that she should sit on one of the cubes)*

BETH: I'm...

CLOWN: *(Firmly)* Thank you!

BETH: *(She sits reluctantly. When she does so she adopts a strong attitude.)* Where is she?

CLOWN: *(Quietly)* Safe

BETH: *(Stands relieved as though she is ready to go)* Where... ?

CLOWN: *(Normal)* And will remain so... *(Indicates that she sits. BETH does so with the same reluctance but more quickly)* Thank you. Until...

BETH: I've brought his cloth.

CLOWN: Cloth?

BETH: *(Reveals a well – grotted piece of red rag)* His comfort. *(CLOWN gives her a quizzical look)* He sucks it. More hygienic than his thumb. Now I'm not sure. So... *(Stands and holds the rag as though wanting the CLOWN to take it)* I'll...

CLOWN: *(After a moment the CLOWN takes the rag)* Thank you *(Also meaning 'sit down'. BETH does so more laboured and less confident than before)* Well?

BETH: *(Seemingly recovered)* I'll take him now. I've come to take him home. *(Suddenly belligerent)* You have absolutely no right whatsoever to...

CLOWN: What gives you the right? *(Pause whilst she awaits a reply. BETH returns a ball. CLOWN catches it and her light brightens.)* Well... ?

BETH: To want, to *demand* my son?
CLOWN: Yes. The right.
BETH: I'm his mother.
CLOWN: That gives you the right?
BETH: Of course.
CLOWN: 'fraid not.
BETH: 'fraid so. There's no reason to keep him against his will.
CLOWN: (*Quietly*) I'm not.
BETH: Don't be stupid!
CLOWN: (*Painted smile*) I can't help it. Catch... (*Tosses an imaginary ball to her. As she attempts to catch it she drops her filofax and the ball, and curses. Light out. CLOWN chuckling*) Butterfingers...
BETH: (*Splitting anger, gathering up her filofax*) Fool!

I'd like to introduce you to someone. Another woman. Another... mother.

18. Joan

(*Tosses ball to the other side of the corridor of light. Caught in the same way as BETH affecting the entrance of JOAN wearing the same institutional gown. She carries a glossy, bulging, handbag. The CLOWN indicates that BETH should pick up the remaining two balls. Something in the Clown's slight movement forward impels her to comply. As she does so she and JOAN are lit. She throws one of the balls to the CLOWN with catches it and indicates the unoccupied cube inviting JOAN to sit on it. She does so, posing legs and smiles*) Joan.

JOAN: Me.
CLOWN: Joan.
JOAN: (*As though knowing the negative response*) Can I smoke?
CLOWN: (*Quietly*) No.
JOAN: (*Adjusts pose*) Go on.

CLOWN: No.
JOAN: (Adjusts again) Just one.
CLOWN: 'fraid not.
JOAN: Oh... ? (*CLOWN remains unmoved*) Fuck off then!!
CLOWN: Joan. (*Pause*) Joan... this is... Beth
JOAN: Fuck off!

CLOWN: I'd like you to meet Beth. (*To BETH*) Beth... (*To JOAN*) Joan. (*JOAN ignores BETH's proferred greeting and opens up her handbag... searching*) Beth is in the same position as you.

JOAN: (*Finding mirror and lipstick. Begins applying*) Don't soft-soap me you piss-'ead.

CLOWN: Exactly. Same.

JOAN: Liar.

CLOWN: True

JOAN: (*Without glancing at BETH*) Never seen 'er before.

CLOWN: I shouldn't imagine so, But she's here for the same reason, and like you she 'doesn't 'like it', doesn't...' deserve it' and isn't going to...' allow it'... like you.

JOAN: 'Ow can she be like me you liar!

CLOWN: (*About to reply but decides against it. Pauses*) I'd like you to get to know each other (*Tosses remaining ball to JOAN. She catches it easily at the expense of the contents of her bag which scatter obout her. Bangles, beads. A theatrical make-up box of tricks*)

JOAN: Shit!!

(*The CLOWN makes a jaunty exit. JOAN gathers up the contents of her bag and bundles them back maintaining the disorder. BETH takes a pencil from the spine of her filofax and begins to write in her 'notes' section.*)

JOAN: (*After say ten seconds*) What you writing?

BETH: Notes

JOAN: What fo'?

BETH: So that I can remember accurately what was said.

JOAN: What fo'?

BETH: (*Patronisingly*) Don't you know?

JOAN: You wha... ?

BETH: Never mind.

JOAN: Go on... (*BETH resumes writing*) No go on, tell me.

BETH: Sorry...

JOAN: Piss off!! (*Begins lining her lips. Long pause*) What did you do? (*BETH continues to write*) 'Said what did you do?! Must've done something else you wouldn't be 'ere (*BETH continues writing*) Not a lot. Can tell. Smell. You stink of nothing. Bet you get out of 'ere before me. Don't stand a chance I don't. Not with my reputation. (*Sees that BETH is still writing*) Waste of time you are. You Snot! (*Closes bag, and rolls the balls over in her hand with surprising agility: Something like a conjurer. She begins juggling. First one and then both balls after a couple of failures she becomes quickly expert. She's done it before. She notices the third ball on BETH's lap*) You need that?

BETH: (*Stopping her writing*) What?

JOAN: That. (*Indicates ball*)

BETH: Why should I need this?

JOAN: So you were listening.

BETH: (*Returning to her filofax*) Oh god...

JOAN: Does that mean you don't (*BETH shrugs unconcerned*) Then chuck it over (*BETH does so. Loses her light. Becomes gradually more inquisitive as she sees JOAN introduce the third ball and then, after a couple of false starts, gains in confidence and goes into a variety of threesome juggling routines*)

BETH: (*Genuinely impressed*) Very good.

JOAN: Easy.

BETH: Doesn't look it.

JOAN: Anyone can do it. Even you.

BETH: Don't think so.

JOAN: Go on. Easy. Therapeutic. Look I'll do it slowly, one at a time. (*Moves towards her, sharing her light. BETH shies away and returns to her filofax*) Please yourself. (*Moves away and begins juggling again. Enter CLOWN. He moves across the front of JOAN and takes over the three balls from her, continuing the juggling without her seemingly being aware of this. Lost, She returns to her chair, her face, her lipstick, eyelashes, earlobes, trinkets... out of light*)

CLOWN: Thank you. (*Referring to balls. JOAN throws them to him*) So... sorted it have you? Found the common factors? (*Both remain engrossed in self*) I see. Well I'll just have to remove myself once again, and leave you – once again – until such time as... erm... here (*Throws a ball into BETH's lap. She is lit instantly and reacts once again with spitting rage. Dropping her filofax and pencil*)

BETH: You imbecillic oaf! How dare you... !

CLOWN: Good! (*Pause for a couple of seconds before tossing one of the remaining balls to JOAN – who is ready for it and catches it, is instantly lit – and begins the previous introductions once again*) Beth... Joan.
Joan... (*Tosses the remaining ball to JOAN, she catches it. CLOWN exits jauntily. Chuckling. JOAN picks up BETH's pencil and hands it to her*)

JOAN: Seen it all before love. Once you've seen one you've seen the lot. Clever little shit. (*BETH sorts out her filofax*) Try that again, and again, and again...

BETH: So...?

JOAN: (*Pause*) Why you 'ere?

BETH: My business.

JOAN: No.

BETH: Meaning?

JOAN: Their business. We stay'ere until... look, this is fucking stupid. You've gorra kid, right?!

BETH: (*Quietly*) Yes.

JOAN: (*Responding. Quietly*) You're 'unfit'. Right?

BETH: No! (*Very quietly*) So they say.

JOAN: So am I – so they say. (*Pause*) 'ow long you been 'ere?

BETH: A week... eight days. Can't believe it. Eighteenth. Today's the eighteenth. A week... eight days ago. (*Opens her filofax, finds the page*) Here. The tenth. (*Reading*) 'Desperate. Hospital.' (*Closes filofax*) Can't believe it.

JOAN: (*Quietly*) I can. They've tried it before. This time they've got me. Found out. What I do? Proof.

BETH: What difference does that make

JOAN: A lot. The reason why I'm 'ere.

BETH: No. What difference does it make, what you do?

JOAN: In my case, everything.

CLOWN: (*Enter very brisk*) Good... communicating, getting to know the whys and wherefores. Fascinating isn't it? So... how far have you... reached? Or have you... Over-reached, is that why I came in when I did, why I'm here? Mmm?

(*Looks at BETH and indicates the she throws to her the ball she is holding. She does so, JOAN likewise. Quickly. Automatic*)

Thank you.
    (*BETH opens her filofax*) Oh, sorry Beth, not this time. I'll have that. (*Indicates the filofax*)

BETH: That's one step too far. There is no way that I am going to give this to you, under any circumstances. You have no rights whatsoever to remove this. Take your silly little games elsewhere.

CLOWN: Quite a mouthfull. Old habits returning. Which means that you still don't believe it. I suppose you thought you could get away with it. Tell her Joan. Now you've started. Tell her. Go on.

JOAN: Where d' you want it?

CLOWN: Slide it (*Indicates handbag*)... out of reach. (*Does so*) That will do. (*JOAN stands and slides her handbag across the floor towards the clown and then sits, hands clasping and unclasping her absent handbag*) Thank you. What advice have you got to give to your new... companion Joan? Mmm?

(*Pause*)

JOAN: Beth...

CLOWN: Good.

JOAN: Beth love (*Pause*) Do as you're told. Give it over. (*BETH ignores her clutching her filofax more tightly*) Look love it's no good doin' that, there's no way you're goin' to keep it if they don't want you to so...

CLOWN: Don't think she's going to Joan. In fact... (*Starts throwing the balls higher and with greater deliberation*)

JOAN: Beth! (*To CLOWN*) Do it yourself, nothin' to do with me you shitbag. (*Angry*) Give us a faaaag... !

CLOWN: (*Laughing. Juggling more relaxed*) Props. How do we cope without them? (*To BETH, indicating filofax*) So... ? (*BETH unmoved*) No... ? Sure... ? Joan... ? Right (*Throws the balls in sequence over BETH who allows them to bounce off her. She smiles at this. So does the CLOWN who slowly removes a large box of matches from a pocket, strikes it...*) So... (*Removes red rag from top pocket and moves to light it*)

BETH: No!! (*Throws the filofax at the CLOWN who remains unmoved as it hits him. Blows out the match*)

CLOWN: (*Retrieving the balls*) Thank you Beth. We all need props. Best not destroy them unless they harm you. (*Pause*) Story time. (*Laughs*)

JOAN: (*Groans*) Shit. (*CLOWN smiles and tosses the three balls to JOAN one at a time*)

I was at it. The lot. Wouldn't stop. Given me the money before 'and so I thought I could cut 'im short. Bring 'im off quick and then gerron wi' the next one, before I 'ad me dinner. Anyway... (*Quick flurry of juggling... say five seconds*) 'E wouldn't. Gerroff. 'n I couldn't shift 'im 'e were so fat, I was at risk. 'e was definitely an 'ealth 'azard. Anyway... (*Another quick flurry*) 'E fell off me, on the floor

(*She drops them in a close pile on the floor. Lights off. Lights on as she is recovering them and putting them in her lap. For the rest of the speech she manipulates the balls to complement and illustrate her narrative. A quick flurry of juggling as before each time she says 'anyway'*)

I laughed, and nipped quick off the end of the bed and started pullin' on me thingies and couldn't stop... laughing. I 'ad to go out. So I made me excuses, checked who me next one was, looked down the staircase and saw that 'e was there... waitin'. So I rushed back in an'... 'e was still there, where 'a left 'im... spread about the carpet like an upturned Walrus, with a Johnny still on 'is dick... just. Well... (*Juggle*)... 'e'd crushed me radio alarm... when 'e fell. So I screamed. There didn't seem anything else left. A mean what would you 'ave done? Anyway... (*Juggles*)

CLOWN: Thank you.
JOAN: Wha'?
CLOWN: Please...

JOAN: Oh... (*Throws him a ball*)

CLOWN: (*Now lit, she throws the balls and goes into darkness*) Get to the end of it.

JOAN: (*Laughing*) You mean the bit where 'e... ?

CLOWN: (*Unsmiling*) No. The *end* of it.

JOAN: The very end?

CLOWN: End. (*Returns one ball*) Now. (*Next ball*) Do it! (*Final ball*)

JOAN: (*Juggling*) They took 'er. Took 'er. Said I wasn't fit. Said that... I was disgusting. Because of what I did, I was disgustin' and wasn't fit. Why am I not fit? I said. Because of what you do they said. But she's delightful... my Popsy. Where d'you learn a word like that? they said. You imagine that. Not only am I a shitty mother in their eyes because I do what I do, I don't understand words, can't use them. Delightful I said. She's delightful. And they agreed – eventually – that she was, is, delightful. Why's that I said? Not because of you they said. Can't be because of you they said. *You're* disgusting. You're disgusting I said. (*Turns to CLOWN*) That's what I said wasn't it?

CLOWN: (*Chuckling*) You certainly did.

JOAN: She loves me. Popsy loves me. I love 'er. Simple. Easy. Beautiful. See, another word. Beautiful. Like delightful. I know what they mean. 'cos I know. So does Popsy. And these... *shits*... there's a word – they KNOW I know what that means – these *shits* think I don't have no right to know. So that's why I'm 'ere. (*Throws one ball to BETH*) Your turn.

BETH: No way. (*Returns the ball*)

CLOWN: Right. (*Lights another match*)

BETH: (*Faltering*) I... Home. Home. Same as you. In the garden. Pottering in the greenhouse actually. Pricking out. (*Clown blows out the match*)

BETH: I... Onions... delicate... I... I...

JOAN: (*Throwing the three balls*) Try these.

BETH: (*She catches them and begins to try to juggle with them, clumsily at first, then stops, calmer*) It's difficult enough. They're so delicate. You have to hold them so gently between your finger, your Forefinger and thumb. Then you hook it out. Looks like a new blade of grass only the black seed still clings to the point, folded. Beautiful.

JOAN: Nothing to do with it. Not why you're 'ere.

CLOWN: Everything to do with it. Listen.

BETH: In he came, right in the middle, no warning, through the door... (*Begins to juggle properly*) and knocks the tray, of pricked-out onions, (*Three balls spring out of her hands onto the floor. Darkness*) off the bench, onto the gravel. (*Stops juggling*) Couldn't believe it. Couldn't believe that he could be so stupid...

CLOWN: Matthew, her son. Eight.

BETH: You stupid boy! You stupid, stupid little shit!! Look at it. All that work. Look at it! Youuuuuu... (*CLOWN picks up balls one by one and the light grows accordingly)*

CLOWN: Took him by his shirt *(Tosses one ball to BETH)* and threw him through the door. *(Pause)* Through it.

BETH: *(Sits. Quietly)* Deserved it. Been brought up to think before he acts; to use his mind. He's a very bright boy but he'd been stepping out of line for a couple of days. Little things like dirtying his clothes, being silly, putting his light on when he's supposed to go to sleep – went through that stage years ago. That sort of thing. Deserved it.

CLOWN: Nasty cut.

BETH: Deserved it. He'll learn.

CLOWN: Did he get pushed around often?

BETH: He gets a hard smack if he steps out of line if that's what you mean? It's a matter of standards. If I make a mistake, I pay for it. I don't make many mistakes. *(Quietly as though not convinced)* Neither will he. Doesn't do any harm. *(Begins weeping quietly)*

CLOWN: Joan? *(Throws ball to JOAN)*

JOAN: And you keep me 'ere from my Popsy an' compare me with 'er. Makes me shiver.

CLOWN: Not quite the same though is it?

JOAN: Never 'it Popsy in my life.

CLOWN: *(Chuckling)* Long life.

JOAN: Don't you come funny with me. I won't ever. Couldn't do it. Can't think why I ever should. 'Ow do you lift your 'ands to someone that you...

CLOWN: Love?

JOAN: That you...

CLOWN: What's the matter Joan? Problem with a word Joan? How many people do You love Joan. Joan?

JOAN: *(Quietly)* Popsy. That's who.

CLOWN: *(Quietly. Smiling)* So... on your feet. *(JOAN complies)* Beth? *(She slowly complies. Still weeping quietly.)* Swap? *(JOAN nods. CLOWN exchanges her handbag for the ball. BETH sees this and does the same for her filofax)* Thank you. *(The CLOWN begins to juggle. This seems to be the signal for BETH and JOAN to gather their belongings and leave. They move their chairs to the left and right centre corners of the square before leaving along the corridors of light from which they entered. They are immediately replaced by HIM and HER, the characters of the final part. They are dressed in judo jackets and trousers. His black, Hers white. HE sits in one corner stage right and SHE in the opposite corner stage left. They should give the sense of being combatants in a ring but not overly so. HE begins applying dubbin to a pair of boots with deep concentration, whilst SHE opens her sketchbook and begins drawing)*

CLOWN: *(Ignoring them, backing towards the corridor of light)* So there you have it. Easy. Switch off. Passing through the air; hardly touching. No contact. If you start to feel what you're touching then it'll all (*Throws one ball into the wings stage left*) fall (*Throws the second ball*) down (*Throws the final ball. Exits slowly stage right. Just as he disappears, the SIBLING masked in the UNBORN's mask, dressed in the same version of the clown costume, enters stage left along the corridor of light, juggling with consummate ease*)

IN TOUCH

CAST

SIBLING   sister to all children
HIM   SIBLING's father
HER   SIBLING's mother married to HIM

CLOWN/SIBLING: I'm the last. (*Drops the balls*) Don't worry about the two before me. We're unrelated, though they have been trying to tie a few things together – casting a few doubts as well. No matter, plenty of time to come to a resolution (*Chuckles*)... If there is one. Anyway. (*Removes her clown costume revealing simple 'blacks' underneath. She then removes her mask*) Me. Then, a while ago. Not even a twinkle yet. These two (*Referring to HIM and HER*) they've not even met – yet. But they're going to. Let me

19. Sibling

introduce them in the language I've learned, using it in... retrospect so to speak. On my right, itching to go, wanting to begin this simple love story is Him (*Indicates HIM*) builder of dry – one walls. Brilliant. On my left (*Indicates HER*) Her, Teacher, just begun her probationary year; a natural. Me...? Poet. Aspiring. (*Smiling*) Watching. Getting it all down in my own style. (*Pause*) The occasion? A gathering, somewhere North. A short time after midnight. New Year. A while ago.

(*The rest of the play resembles the form and ritual of a wrestling match. The corners offer a sanctuary, a base to return to. hilst in the corners there is much preparation, much advice, much repair, much to reflect upon as each round unfolds and passes. The SIBLING acts as referee and*

55

second to each combatant. As the SIBLING retreats to a central space slightly upstage of HIM and HER, The SIBLING appears to call them together like a referee. HIM and HER stand and take a tentative step forward eyes becoming fixed, as though there is a compulsion to greet each other.)

20. Him

21. Her

HER: Hello...
SIBLING: She said.
HIM: Hello...
HIM: Hello...
SIBLING: He said.
  And they both stood apart and waited
  For the other to...
  Repeat what they'd said
HIM: Hello...
SIBLING: She said.
HIM: Hello...
SIBLING: He said
  As many times as it to took get used to
  Saying...
ALL: Hello.
SIBLING: And in this first greeting, at the annual
  celebration,
  Where the dry misty tissue

Is left in a crackling heap
Discarded in favour of the
Brilliant, glistening, New,
Unnoticed
Imperceptible...
Two grinning cheeks
Dimpled together
and said...

(HIM and HER go through a gentle laughing sequence of ritualistic sparring before...)

HER: Hello.
HIM: *(Pause)* Happy New Year
HER: Happy New Year *(They both laugh nervously not quite knowing what to do even though – within the tradition of the celebration – they have licence to at least embrace. They look around desperate for assistance or a distraction, yet not quite wanting one)*
SIBLING: *(Chuckling)* What now? How to proceed? This is the moment they've grown for. Ripe. Weeks ago since it began. Weeks since they learned to watch and pass on silly signals. Now, when they've every excuse to break the glass and sift the sand, they don't know what to do *(Smiles)* – or think they don't.

(During the next sequences the two pass through the same ritualistic sparring. Slowly. An element at a time, complementing each speech.)

HER: Your parents here?
HIM: Yes.
HER: Did you come with them?
HIM: Er... no.
HER: You sound doubtful.
HIM: No...
HER: You do...
HIM: No...
HER: *(Smiling)* You're lying.
HIM: I'm not...
HER: You are, I can tell
HIM: I walked.
HER: Don't believe you.
HIM: Why should I lie?
HER: It's miles.
HIM: It's a beautiful night.

HER: It's freezing!

HIM: Beautiful. I like walking.

HER: I can't stand walking. (*Pause*) I still don't believe you. Saw you come in with them.

HIM: I didn't. We met in the car park. Coincidence

HER: (*Quieter*) Don't believe you.

HIM: (*Pause*) Happy New Year. (*Turns and goes back to his corner and begins applying dubbin to his boots once more, whilst she re-appraises her face*)

SIBLING: And the words that came a-flowing against the curl of the tongue, spitting at random out of their mouths, out of control... Meaningless. Not a grain of truth in the accusation or the lies. (*Pause*) Time to ponder a minute. Listen to their heads for a second or two in the empty air, instead of the flapping of their hearts. Try again. For there's still no one looking. Even They're not looking. (*Chuckles*) At least they're pretending not to!

HER: (*To Sibling*) Why did I do that?

SIBLING: You did.

HIM: (*To Sibling*) What was all that about?

SIBLING: (*Laughing*) Don't you know?

HIM: Not a clue. She called me a liar. That's the first time I've spoken to her.

SIBLING: (*Laughing*) With words.

HIM: With me!

HER: What you laughing at?

SIBLING: Both of you.

BOTH: Why?

SIBLING: You hang around each other's eyes like searching humming birds. If you stay like that for too long you'll grow tired and kick your wings towards other juices. (*Chuckles*) Now it's me who's floating a lie. The fact is, you have no choice. What you've started in your own style, is the beginning of me. And here (*Refers to the arena*) is where it shall continue. So discover it (*Chuckles*) if you haven't already. Ready?

HER: No way.

SIBLING: Why not?

HER: I was so... well he wouldn't after what I said. I don't know why I said it, kept accusing him like that. He wouldn't want to know.

SIBLING: He will.

HER: How can you be so sure?

SIBLING: I'm sure.

HER: What should I do?

SIBLING: Instinct. Follow it.

HER: I'm going home!

SIBLING: (*Laughing*) No, you're not (*She is gently 'frozen' in mid-stride*)

HIM: Where's she going?
SIBLING: Does it matter?
HIM: No.
SIBLING: Mind you're own business then .
HIM: No problem
SIBLING: Fine
HIM: She insulted me
SIBLING: Fine
HIM: Called me a liar, I've never lied in my life!
SIBLING: Liar.
HIM: I'm going!
SIBLING: So's she.
HIM: Now. Home!
SIBLING: So's she.
HIM: What?
SIBLING: That's where she's going. Home.
HIM: She's not!
SIBLING: You could be right. (*HIM and HER repeat their ritual exchange as before only with much more energy and much more of a flourish at its conclusion. Warming up*)
HIM: Where you going?
HER: Home.
HIM: But why?
HER: Mind you're own business... (*Sees HIM begin to join the ritual like the Raven dance in Losing Touch. He speaks some of the key words like 'nervous, it's never happened like this before'... simultaneously*) and I didn't mean that I don't know why I keep doing that to you when its the last thing I want to do want to do at all and I'm so nervous that I can't seem to get any of it sorted in my head and so I keep I keep I keep and it's never happened like this before but before I've always been shat on and I don't want want want want to...
HIM: I do...
HER: Want to want to...
HIM: I do...
HER: (*Laughing suddenly very calm*) I knew you would.
HIM: (*Smiling*) How d'you know?
HER: Couldn't possibly tell you.
HIM: Go on...
HER: Couldn't possibly
HIM: Because you don't know.
HER: Do.
HIM: No way.
HER: Do.

HIM: Liar.

HER: (*Quietly smiling*) Liar (*Both engage in a slow, laughing version of the dance, ending up holding each other at arm's length before they embrace*)

SIBLING: (*To audience*) I think I'm going to be sick (*Chuckles*) at least she is. It doesn't take long does it, if it's right? Funny thing is, these two ravens didn't want to wheel and deal for very long. All of a rush. Everywhere. They didn't even bother to check time before each other; (*Pause*) And so it was I became the twinkle in both their eyes, and they laughed, and grew careless, and forgot, and remembered, too late. (*HIM and HER separate and return to their corners*) And he didn't know what was wrong – or rather, what was right.

HIM: What's wrong?

SIBLING: Nothing

HIM: Something is.

SIBLING: You're wrong.

HIM: Well look at her (*Without looking*) She's different.

SIBLING: That's because of us.

HIM: What've you got to do with it?

SIBLING: Because I am.

HIM: I don't understand.

SIBLING: Simple. (*Goes towards HIM laughing, sits on his knee removing shoes and polish*) Dad!

HIM: What?

SIBLING: You're my dad

HIM: (*Pushing SIBLING gently off his knee he goes to HER corner and draws HER to the centre of the arena with an almost angry version of the dance*) Why didn't you tell me?

HER: Because I didn't...

HIM: That's no answer... (*They move, to another corner*)

HER: I didn't know.

HIM: Come on...

HER: I didn't. How am I supposed to know, eh? How? *you'll* never know so how am I supposed to know? what a clever clever you try to be sometimes. I know what I'm *supposed* to know, but I don't *know*. (*Pause. Quietly*) But I do now. I feel sick.

SIBLING: And she was. Often.

HIM: Anything I can do?

HER: Yes.

HIM: What?

HER: Leave me alone.

SIBLING: And me...

HIM: If that's what you want.

HER: I do.

SIBLING: She didn't.

HIM: If that's what you want.

HER: I don't.

HIM: What?

SIBLING: (*Sharply*) She doesn't! (*Ritual dance this time in shorthand, abbreviated, until – at its conclusion – a long embrace accounting for the new bulge and accommodating posture. Separating the two slowly, smiling*)
And their tears fell together. And there I was, a limpet clinging to, feeding off, the rough underbelly, growing incessantly, staring death in the mouth – blindly; hugging myself within the swishing tides of this hanging new-mooned sac. And I grew oblivious of the this and that of the time to come, but learning much from her, sharing her with him

(*Moves into a position where she can break their embrace*)

And their tears fell together, swelling the solitary tear under her breasts until... (*Easing them gently apart; the birth*) until it burst beneath her... (*Taking HER with her. HIM hovers and watches uncertain... A semblance of the referee*)

HIM: (*Delighted. Cooing*) A girl.

SIBLING: Very observant.

HER: Knew it.

HIM: (*Laughing*) Liar. (*Goes to collect towel*)

HER: (*Laughing*) Liar.

HIM: Who's a clever girl then?

HER: (*New ritual of handling the baby, passing the SIBLING between them. Kisses and hugs. Towels used to wipe and caress the SIBLING's hands, face etc*) She is.

HIM: You are.

HER: We are... (*Eventually after much handling*)

SIBLING: I think I'm going to be sick!

(*Ritual changes gradually from complete joy to one of extreme concern. SIBLING now ill. HER comforting, wiping brow with towel. HIM looking on.*)
And I was. Very.

HER: She's not right.

HIM: But the doctor couldn't find anything.

HER: She's not right.

SIBLING: I know.

HIM: Then do something.

SIBLING: Yes. Please.

HER: I have.

SIBLING: Tired. Arms. Can't move them.

HER: (*Besides herself with anxiety*) She's not right!

HIM: What shall we do?

SIBLING: Very tired.

HER: Have to take her. Put her in front of them... on the desk, anything, and scream and shout until...

SIBLING: Yes.

HIM: Right. Now. Let's go.

HER: Now!

SIBLING: So we went. (*Towel used as bed sheet*) And so I was pulled and pricked and bled, and so I grew more and more tired as I lost all reason to scream... all brightness gone. And so... and so... (*Towel being pulled slowly over Sibling's face implying imminent death. Desperately worried parents waiting around their sibling, sick with concern and drenched with a willingness for its survival*) and so... ? (*Towel pulled over and away from SIBLING's head. SIBLING smiles brightly. Laughing*) I lived! Septicaemia. Body rotten with it. Diagnosed. Treated. No harm done. Much good. My parents – Him and Her – so relieved. New dimension. So much in love. So much. And we all became quite revolting in our love for each other.

(*Towel draped on the floor and used as both nappy and baby-bouncer, sibling being suspended in towel by HIM and HER*)

22. Scene from *In Touch*

And I was so happy as I shat and spewed and gurgled and bawled and dribbled and teethed and weaned and screamed and Mummy'd and Daddy'd yes'd, no'd and refused to know what they meant until I wanted to, and woke them and kissed them missed them, pissed on them and and... (*Brief exchange between them all showing the trials and joys of a new family*) and loved them. (*Settled down on the floor*) I really learned how to love them. And they (*Indicates HIM and HER who have launched into an embrace*)... my parents, equally so (*Laughing*) So embarrassing it was revolting. Always at it; touching and things. Wherever we went – and even if we didn't – they were (*Look of extreme disgust*) at it! (*Quick exchange of touching. Pause. Surprised.*) Oh. Work. (*Snaps towel to break up the embrace. He prepares for his work and she returns to her corner to muse*) Nearly forgot. Plenty of that, even in winter. Probably more so for my Dad. For Mum an urge to get back to it; renew the struggle, the confrontation with the children of others; and yet almost not daring to. The reason for their first big argument. (*Moves to HIM corner folding the towel and leaving it upon the box*) Whether to leave me with Meg down the road – and Mum return to teaching – or for Mum to resign and stay at home; Dad looking after me never came into it. He was with his walls... (*Stands with legs slightly astride close to the box in HIM's corner, facing HER who is similarly positioned beside her box*) always.

HIM: (*Fighting the cold, but gradually warming as the task warms*) Bitter. Not enough to freeze the cockles but... glad I put in the foundations last night. Didn't used to. Slower in the mornings at the moment. Be all right once I get going. Best bit is when I don't have to think. Definitely the best bit. Empty head and start again. Let it all come in and then tease it out, with the day. (*Stretches a line knee-height across the centre of the space attached to one leg of Her and Sibling*) Five strides. On average that's about a mile a year; mile an' a quarter if I'm lucky an' don't knacker my back with anything. So I count miles of walls as years. My working life is as long as a wall. The wall around this field will take this winter. Four or five months... depending. (*Pause*) Won't be long before I'm spotting them before I bend. Save my back and time. After a while you can see what you want even though it's random stone; long before. See the 'throughs', spot the 'copes' almost as you get to them. One over two, two over one; empty your head and run... (*Shudders with cold*).

SIBLING: She wanted to. (*Folds up line approaching HER. HIM sits in his corner*) Only she couldn't; she was with me, resenting it. Resenting him as well when she really wanted to run... and couldn't. (*Settles on her lap*)

HER: (*Cooing*) What am I going to do now my little shitbag? Well I'm not going to do much I can tell you. You're going to bore me out of my skull, all day long. Yes you are gorgeous little shitbag. I know you're very beautiful because your Daddy's very very beautiful and I know that at sometime today I'm going to have to feed you and feed me and feed him and feed us and feed you again and again and again... but I do wish I was at school my sweet, darling little shitbag... I really do. (*Pause*) And I shouldn't have done it.

SIBLING: And I didn't understand. They seemed to be laughing at each other. That was the problem; they were laughing at rather than with. (*Pause*) Breakfast.

(*Rushes across to him. Lifts him to his feet, and tosses the towel over one of his shoulders*)

Boiled eggs. Toasted soldiers.

(*HIM takes the towel and drapes it like a bib around SIBLING who has set herself on the corner box of HIM centre stage. SHE remains in her corner*)

HER: Why do you always do that?
HIM: What?
HER: Cut your toast into soldiers?
HIM: Always done it.
HER: But why?
HIM: Because. In the family. The way we do it. Great.
HER: You mean it's hereditary?
HIM: No. I mean it's in the family. They did it, I do it and she'll do it.
HER: Why? (*Laughing*) It's disgusting.
HIM: (*Laughing. Making his mouth mock-grotesquely over-full*) It's luscious! Isn't it love (*Offers a soldier to SIBLING. Still at a distance*)
SIBLING: (*Laughing*) Yes...
HER: (*Laughing*) No.
HIM: (*Laughing*) She loves it don't you love?
SIBLING: Me want.
HIM: (*Standing and teasing SIBLING with another dipped 'soldier' much encouraged by the favourable response*) Another?
SIBLING: (*Nodding*) Mmmm.
HER: (*Smiling*) No.
HIM: Right. (*Quietly. Looking at HER, marching the 'soldier'*) Soldier's marching with the cart, trying not to break a fart, toasted soldier big as me finger, hope the smelly fart won't linger...
HER: Don't !
HIM: Close your eyes.
SIBLING: (*Half closes them squealing with delight*) Am
HIM: No peeping.
SIBLING: (*Eyes tightly scrunched*) Am
HER: (*Definitely not smiling now*) stop it.

HIM: Ready... ?

SIBLING: Am

HIM: Open wide and... into the egg (*Much clucking accompaniment*) and... into you mouth. (*Pretends that SIBLING has bit his finger*) Aaaaaaaaaaagh! (*Much exaggerated pain and shaking of hand*)

HER: Enough. Stop it.

HIM: Where's it gone?

SIBLING: (*Indicating mouth*) Me.

HIM: (*Making exaggerated forays into SIBLING's mouth. Pretending to look deep into her stomach*) Where?

SIBLING: Me.

HIM: In there?

SIBLING: Yes.

HIM: My finger?

SIBLING: (*Laughing*) Yes.

HIM: Let's have it then?

SIBLING: Can't.

HIM: Got to. Look. (*Shows space in hand where finger used to be*) Right.

SIBLING: Can't. Eaten it.

HIM: Right! (*Rolls up sleeve of his shirt on the arms of the missing finger. Much exaggerated play of preparing to plunge the hand and arm down into the mouth down into the stomach of the SIBLING*) Now then. What I'm going to do is...

SIBLING: No

HIM: (*Another quick flurry of action*) No what I'm going to do is...

SIBLING: No...

HIM: No (*Abbreviated version of action. Speech is punctuated by many "no's" and "daddy's" from SIBLING and "stop it's" from HER*)
I'm going to... Yes that's what I'll do I'll put my hand in there (*Indicates mouth*) go through there down there in there feel around a bit and hope that you didn't chew it because if you did I'll never find it that's what I'm going to do so a – one, a – two, and a, no 'ang on a minute I've got a better idea, I think I'm going to dive in there yes that's what I'm going to... do before I put my socks and boots on. Ready?.

(*Stands well away and makes elaborate preparations to dive measuring distances trajectory etc*).

A – one, a – two and a – threeeeeeeeeeeeeeeee!

HER: STOP IT!

HIM: eeeeeeeeeee.

HER: (*Rushing to SIBLING*) Stop it stop it stop it!! (*He does. Pause. SIBLING's laughter changes to a cry*) Now see what you've done.

HIM: (*Quietly*) Me?

HER: You, you fool! Look at the state of her.

23. Scene from *In Touch*

HIM: I was making her laugh. You stopped that.

HER: (*SIBLING crying loudly now*) Look at the state. Nearly choking. No need. Stupid!

HIM: All right. (*Sits down. Begins polishing his boots*) Got to go.

(*Pause*)

HER: Don't go.

HIM: You must be joking.

HER: Don't.

HIM: (*Quietly*) Bit of fun. Bit of laughter. Words. Fart. That's where it began isn't it? A silly word which makes me laugh, which she (*Indicating SIBLING*) doesn't understand, and she won't use it anyway if you've got anything to do with it... even though you do as well

HER: What?

HIM: (*Back to boots. Quietly*) Fart.

HER: No I don't. Disgusting !

HIM: Yes you do. And you're not alone you'll be surprised to know. So don't go around telling everyone that you've married an oddbod. I'm not the only one. (*Starts laughing*)

HER: (*Not knowing whether to laugh or cry*) You did that on purpose.

HIM: (*Laughing. pleading innocence*) Me? (*Turns to SIBLING*) Daddy's not an oddbod is he?
HER: You're crude.
HIM: Me?
HER: You.
HIM: Getaway... (*Goes to SIBLING*) I'm not crude am I love? Open wide. (*Offers the last of the egg*) Good girl. Right. Got to go to work now my lovely egg-filled chopsy...
HER: So have I...
HIM: So has Mummy.
HER: Night shift over, day shift begun.
HIM: (*Quietly*) See you at the night shift then.
HER: When will that be?
HIM: When I've walled another five paces.

(*They both hint that they're about to go into a ritual of 'goodbye for the day' but don't and settle wearily in their corners*)

SIBLING: And she did, eventually, go back to school. He never stood in her way. Encouraged her. And he learned the art of survival (*Chuckles*) in the kitchen (*She hands him the towel which he folds as he sits in her corner. Serious*) and in his heart.

(*SHE moves to his corner and begins applying dubbin on his boots*)

And she learned to accommodate the ripeness and richness of both his language and of other things. And me? Well. I write it all down now that I've lived through it. It's the only way I'll be able to recall the detail. But not the memory. I've lived the memory. (*Pause*) So what now?

(*Walks slowly with a simple sense of ritual mirroring the walking sequence of the SHEPHERD in 'Losing Touch'*)

Here, in this. (*Indicates the acting area*) where anything can happen, anything you like, it's time for the final story. The end of it. These two (*Indicates HIM and HER*) almost done. Given everything to embrace this (*Indicates the acting arena*) and me. The question I pose is... am I richer for having been here, in this, than if I hadn't . And when they come back, to check on this and me – and they will with amazing regularity and in many a guise – will they rejoice or will they beat me like they've never done in their little life? They've no choice, and neither have I. We've both got to see it through. How do you think they'll finish it? (*Introducing for the last time, touching hands for the last time*) Him... and Her.

(Final dance. Slow but still technically perfectly smooth. The most graceful and dignified yet. From where they sit. Almost the end of their life.)

HIM: You know what?
HER: What?
HIM: You never saw me build a wall.
HER: But I can still see the walls you built.

(Pause)

HER: You know what?
HIM: What?
HER: You never saw me teach.
HIM: But I know most of the kids you taught. *(Pause)* You know what?
HER: What?
HIM: You're quite the most beautiful person I've known in my life.
HER: Thank you. *(Pause)* And you're the ugliest.
HIM: *(Laughing)* You're right.
HER: I know I'm right. *(Pause)* Only one thing left to say. Always wanted to say it, I'm sorry I have to but I'm afraid that it has to be said... *(They go through a barely imperceptable ritual, laugh, and embrace)*
SIBLING: And with that

(HIM and HER return to their corners)

> They gathered their remnants
> and put them carefully together
> So that I could make sense of them.
> He, his boots
> A scuffed mould of toecap and instep
> circled with dubbin and spittle,
> And she, her sketchbook,
> Folding over
> Her wheeling world of thumbing
> and throwing...

(Having gathered their 'bits' HIM and HER exit together)

SIBLING: (*Laughing*) And left me to get on with it.
Leaving me, as I began,
after such a little while
with no choice.

24. Curtain: *Touch* Trilogy

INDEX

www.ingramcontent.com/pod-product-compliance
Ingram Content Group UK Ltd.
Pitfield, Milton Keynes, MK11 3LW, UK
UKHW010021280225
455677UK00023B/733